Salvatore Zofrea
IMAGES FROM THE PSALMS

Salvatore Zofrea

IMAGES FROM THE PSALMS

Ted Snell

FOREWORD BY
EDMUND CAPON

CRAFTSMAN HOUSE

First published in 1992 by Craftsman House BVI Ltd, Tortola, BVI
Distributed in Australia by Craftsman House,
20 Barcoo Street,
Roseville East, NSW 2069, Australia

Distributed internationally through the following offices:

USA	UK	ASIA
STBS Ltd.	STBS Ltd.	STBS (Singapore) Pte Ltd
PO Box 786	5th Floor, Reading Bridge House	Kent Ridge
Cooper Station	Reading Bridge Approach	PO Box 1180
New York	Reading RG1 8PP	Singapore 9111
NY 10276	England	Republic of Singapore

ISBN 976 8097 23 X

Design concept and artwork   *Netan Pty Limited, Sydney*
Typesetter   *Netan Pty Limited, Sydney*
Printer   *Kyodo, Singapore*

This book is dedicated to the memory of my parents
and to my beloved Stephanie Claire
for all the help she has given me
SALVATORE ZOFREA

… and to Jacob, my first born
TED SNELL

CONTENTS

FOREWORD

THE WORK OF Salvatore Zofrea is immensely distinctive. It refutes any attempt at categorisation within a traditional Australian context, simply because Zofrea has retained those flavours and nuances, those sensibilities and enthusiasms, of his native Italy. That is not to say that he is painting pictures that might as well have emerged from Milan or Palermo, or his native Calabria, nor indeed that he has not been touched by his Australian environment, for he clearly has. What is so wonderful and so refreshing about his work is that it owes nothing, except to his own being and his own visions. There is none of the tokenism nor the furtive glancing at perceived peers that is, inevitably I suppose, endemic in so much contemporary art.

I am, for example, quite unable to think of another artist of our age who has adopted the unlikely theme of the Psalms with such a colourful and idiosyncratic determination as Salvatore Zofrea. He is certainly unusual, a latter day commentator, a pervasive voyeur with an eternal twinkle in his eye, of all the sensitivities, emotions, aspirations, the darks and the lights of the human condition that echo through the parables of the Psalms, immortalised in the most colourful, often dogmatic, sometimes melancholic, but sharply sympathetic paintings. Who indeed would have thought the Psalms could have concealed in their wisdom such incisive, witty, poignant, sensuous and indelibly human moments as Zofrea has created for us?

It is this compendium of humanity, a sense of history, faith, belief, imagery that echoes *quattrocento* Italy as it does contemporary urban Australia, that Zofrea manipulates into a thoroughly urbane and present-day idiom. Above all he is a commentator on the human condition and he is, thus, essentially a figurative painter. But the people of his paintings are like icons, symbols of everything from sleaze to saintliness, they are sharply even heavily defined; they are permanent, frozen, inflexible but instilled with human instinct and sympathy, from tenderness to nervousness, from downright shiftiness to the calm repose of solace.

It is perhaps part of the general strangeness of Zofrea's paintings that a first reaction to them can be confused and ambivalent, simply because of the myriad of symbols, historical, contemporary and personal, and the stylistic echoes of the past that mingle with present-day images and aesthetics. It is amusingly disturbing that in compositions of such deliberate construction, strength and seeming solidity, the human frailties are so poignantly expressed through the nuances and subtleties of the dynamics of the emotive tensions and reactions created by Zofrea in his players.

Ultimately, it is the contradiction, even the contest, between faith and instinct, that is the inevitably secular character of our present day environment and our wordly and material pleasures and aspirations, that is so sustaining and intriguing in Zofrea's works. There is a wonderful, slightly cockeyed, even whimsical ambiguity in the ordinary people who throng his canvases, particularly the *Psalms* series, with an almost holy presence. Symbols of a faith that has been discarded or forgotten, is sometimes fragmentarily recalled, but cannot be written out of our psyche. There are constant echoes of conscience, of our vulnerability in the conflict between the perceptions of right and wrong, and the rolling, gathering storm of desire.

That such explorations of good and evil in the circus of life, strongly evident in the *Psalms* series, should be expressed in a manner that might be described as the visual arts equivalent to Fellini, is Zofrea's distinctive contribution. It is not so much just a contribution to Australian art, his visions defy such parochialism; and his style, so colourful, so poignant, so base and yet so invigorating and truthful, echoes the larger than life spirit of a very human and passionate painter.

Edmund Capon
Director,
Art Gallery of New South Wales

ACKNOWLEDGMENTS

No book of this kind could ever be said to be the work of one individual alone. Many people have contributed to the realisation of this project in a multitude of ways and I would like to express my sincere gratitude to all those who have assisted me in the two and a half years of its production.

In particular I would like to thank Salvatore for his generosity in providing whatever information I sought and in giving so freely of his time. The book could not have been written without his full cooperation and he gave it unstintingly.

Stephanie Claire also assisted in so many ways that I must acknowledge my gratitude to her and thank her for support and encouragement that never waned.

A most profound debt of gratitude is owed to Annette Larkin at Macquarie Galleries, for her excellent work in establishing the provenance and exhibition history of all of the works, and to Eileen Chanin whose support was unequivocal.

Over the past three years I have been fortunate to have been able to call upon Kevin Robertson to assist me with the research for several projects I had undertaken. His scrupulous attention to detail and initiative in scanning material has been so valuable that I cannot imagine how I would have completed them without him.

I am also fortunate to be apart of such an exciting team of academics working within the School of Visual Arts at Curtin University of Technology, in Western Australia. In particular my colleagues in the Visual Culture Research Unit, Julian Goddard and Marco Marcon, have provided invaluable practical support and encouragement over the years I have worked on this project.

Research funding from Curtin University of Technology supplemented the research and preparation of this book and I am extremely grateful for that support.

Colleagues in other institutions have also provided me with information and I feel very privileged to have been able to call upon their expertise. Sister Veronica Brady from the Faculty of Arts in the University of Western Australia has been a pillar of support (though she may not know it) and Jody Fitzhardinge from the Department of Italian in the same University is a valued colleague and dear friend. Rob Pascoe from the Fitzroy Institute of Technology also gave generously of his time and experience.

Many other individuals also assisted me in the realisation of this project and at the risk of omitting anyone, I would like to pay special thanks to Joy Legge, Peter Fay, Nevill Drury, Ben Joel, Anna Bosman and Helen Bond.

The debt I owe to Antonia Syme and Mark Dodson is of an entirely different order. Friendship is given freely and welcomed openly, nevertheless, I could not condone the publication of this book without acknowledging publicly the importance of their friendship and its contribution to this book.

Finally I would like to thank my wife Mary Moore, for whom this and other projects must often seem like intruders in our lives. Throughout the years of gestation, research and writing she lives with these lodgers and accommodates them with remarkable forbearance. I can never thank her adequately for her unconditional support and her encouragement.

Salvatore Zofrea in his studio (Photograph: Greg Weight)

TRIALS AND REDEMPTION

THE FIRST FIFTY PSALMS OF SALVATORE ZOFREA

AT A TIME of great personal suffering Salvatore Zofrea was introduced to the Book of Psalms. This anthology of Hebrew poetry contains vows, meditations, laments and prayers designed to be sung during temple worship and then internalised as an instructional guide to everyday living. Their central message that each individual must pass through the trials of life before achieving redemption sustained him during that crisis in his own life and led to his promise to paint all of the 150 Psalms as a thanks for grace received.

In many Italian churches, the faithful make paintings or small offerings inscribed with the initials PGR (Per Gracia Ricevuta — for grace received) after their prayers have been answered. This series of the First Fifty Psalms could well be inscribed PGR.

Salvatore Zofrea was born in the Calabrian village of Borgia on the 24th September, 1946. He was the youngest in a family of ten children, depleted to eight by the early deaths of two of his siblings[1]. He arrived in Australia on the 19th April, 1956 to be met by his father who had left Italy to work in Australia seven years previously. His story is not unique, it is the experience of many migrant families transplanted from one life and forced to undergo the trial of relocation in another land and another culture.

What is significant in this story is that Salvatore Zofrea has made his life and his faith the subject of his art. Throughout this series of paintings the events of his life and his memories of his childhood in Borgia become the vehicle for his meditations on the central questions of existence. The Psalms are a structuring device through which he can approach those questions and explore his own theology because they not only celebrate God but act as a model for righteous behaviour. Consequently they are also cautionary, detailing the dire consequences of any failure to maintain these teachings and in this sense they are both punitive and celebratory. This duality is central to the artist's treatment of the themes embodied in the Psalms and any attempt to neatly precis his theology would be foolhardy. The *Psalms* are a personal exploration of life by an artist whose Italian heritage and Catholicism are central but not the sole pillars of his philosophy. In this sense they are not religious pictures that preach a particular dogma, instead they present a world in which the everyday is imbued with spiritual significance and the commonplace is recast as the site of metaphysical discourse.

GENESIS

IN 1975 ZOFREA was hospitalised with fibrosis and during a long convalescence a friend suggested he should read the Psalms. Living at home in the supportive environment of his parents' house he began painting the first of his meditations on the Old Testament praise-songs as a way of focussing his energies and redirecting his life.

His early work had been rooted in the tradition of European Expressionism. Colour was applied with verve and he moved paint around the canvas with great energy as a response to his intuition about the subject he was describing. The artist in this situation acts as a seismograph, recording every pulse of feeling with great spontaneity[2] as he explores the relationships between people and their environ-

Photograph: Willie Mobbs

ments. At this time Zofrea was placing individuals in dramatic situations in which the full allegorical implication of the narrative flowed over into the objects that surround the central characters.

Success came early with a solo exhibition at Macquarie Galleries in 1967, followed by 13 more in the next ten years. Critical acknowledgment was mixed and influential writers such as Daniel Thomas, Elwyn Lynn and Alan McCulloch urged a certain caution. Thomas was the most disparaging:

> Salvatore Zofrea is an incredibly old-fashioned young painter, thick turgid knifings of figure and landscape out of Van Gogh and Soutine. I can't come to grips with them. Maybe they're all right[3].

Both Lynn and McCulloch saw dangers in this mode of working for a young Australian artist, with Lynn suggesting that:

> Zofrea lets the expressive horse that is by no means an old grey mare have its head, though he tries to ride in too many directions, having something of the heady exuberance of Nolde, the ecstasy of Van Gogh, the death-throe convulsions of Soutine, and occasionally some of Kokoshka's mannered dash and ease … Zofrea has lots of problems, not the least being that he works in a mode now only generally esteemed in the hands of Perceval, Arthur Boyd and Nolan, but then he's a mere 22[4].

and McCulloch pointing out the dangers of easy success:

> In picking his hedonistic way between Bonnard and Soutine or Nolde, the twenty six year old Salvatore Zofrea treads a primrose path to swift success. At present as seeming smooth as the inside of a Ferrari upholstered in leopard skin the path could collapse under the weight of premature advancement. Zofrea should therefore pause and take careful stock of his equipment and potential[5].

These cautionary reviews were not wasted on the young artist and while a trip to Europe in 1971 confirmed his enthusiasm for van Gogh and Soutine, the opportunity to see a wide range of work from very different artists in museums and galleries in Spain, England, Holland and France provided the catalyst to move away from spontaneous gestural expressionism. In particular the fantastic paintings of Hieronymus Bosch offered new narrative possibilities and dealt with the universal concerns of sin, spiritual joy, death, and redemption.

Back in Australia he began exploring these possibilities in paintings that pay direct homage to Bosch. *Seven Deadly Sins* is an allegorical narrative in which symbolic elements enmesh with human figures in an expansive landscape. It is an essay on the corruption of humanity that offers the artist full scope to explore the central questions of existence. The more detailed depiction of the individual elements that make up the universe are somewhat paradoxically introduced into a more expansive world view. His viewpoint has changed to a more distanced, all encompassing vision yet he is drawn to the intricate patterns of growth in a leaf or shell. *Waiting for the Barbarians* uses similar devices to construct a teeming world of incongruities and grotesqueries. This combination of ideas and viewpoints opens up numerous possibilities for communication with the viewer. In particular the confrontation of the central character in this painting, who stares out at us from 'the still point of the turning world'. Amidst the chaos he engages us in a calm and rational personal dialogue. This idea recurs throughout the paintings of the Psalms, indicating a shift in the artist's approach to the viewers of his works.

Expressionist painting presupposes an empathy between the viewer and the painting in which colour, shape, line, distortions of form, rhythm and movement prompt a sympathetic response. This reaction is based upon their own experiences and the process therefore enables the viewer to find correspondences between the artists' world view and their own. While this level of understanding is still important to Zofrea, a more direct appeal to the viewer as a rational human being, able to ponder on the significance of the ideas and images presented, introduces an crucial element in the preparation for his work on the Psalms.

Another key painting of this early period is *The Child Buddha in the Garden*, painted in 1974. Literature and the world of ideas had become increasingly important to the artist and through reading the works of Hermann Hesse an interest in Zen Buddhism was awakened. The narrative techniques of literature proved to be a lasting influence in his construction of images and the view of nature offered through his interest in Zen was another significant linchpin in his preparation for the paintings of the Psalms. The idea that through painting the artist could identify with nature in a harmonious blending that ruptured the distinctions between the external world and his experience was a way of charging the painting with a universal significance. Through a direct correspondence with natural forms he felt that he could suggest the larger truths of existence. The success of this programme was confirmed by Eneide Mignacca writing in *Nation Review*:

> Nature is felt by Zofrea not as a physical reality but as a psychological objective, as the goal of an affective urge. In its pictorial metamorphosis it becomes a kind of impersonal and maternal lover, the source of primeval peace, the seat of equilibrium of all cosmic forces. These pictures leave no doubt that the creator of such splendidly voluptuous nature is the goddess of harmonious tenderness not a paternalistic, authoritarian god[6].

His painting of the young Buddha surrounded by exotic plants, birds and insects suggests a harmony and fruitfulness that goes beyond the particular details of stamens, pistils and leaves to speak of a universal sense of order. At the same time the essential simplicity of Zen thinking was in tune with his own struggle to simplify his technique. The spontaneity of gesture and the rich accretions of paint used in the earlier works were increasingly replaced with carefully constructed surfaces and solidly realised forms. He restricted his palette and gave physical and spiritual weight to his figures through a layered build up of thinly applied veils of colour.

The year after the completion of this painting, Zofrea was in hospital. It was a time for assessment and in the period which followed he redrew the parameters of his life in tandem with a return to the faith of his childhood. His illness highlighted the tenuous nature of human existence and drew him back to Christianity and the Catholic Church. The first painting in this series brings many of these ideas together and sets the course for the artist's exploration of themes uncovered in the early Psalms.

IN THE GARDEN

NATURE IS A central character in several of Zofrea's Psalms, but unlike many Australian artists his version of the natural world is a tended garden. The wild, untrammeled bush holds no allure or any deep significance for him. Although artists as well known as Arthur Boyd and Sidney Nolan have been able to use the impenetrable undergrowth and the vast expanses of red desert as convincing metaphors for pain, suffering and redemption[7], the uncultivated Australian landscape is never nominated as a site for Zofrea's meditations on the message of the Psalms. Instead, it is the inhabited and cultivated hills around Kurrajong where the artist lives and, most often, a garden of flowers, which acts as the crucible for his ideas on the relationship between humanity and the natural environment. They recur throughout the *Psalms* as the setting for both solitary communion and social activity. The first painting in the series begins with an image of God the gardener tending his flowers, introducing the symbolic reading of the garden as representative of earthly and heavenly paradise. The garden is a metaphor for the primal, sin free, condition of humanity, before the fall from grace, and its wider significance as an image of cosmic order gives it a particular potency for Zofrea. After working in an Expressionist mode for more than a decade he focussed his attention on the structure of natural forms in his desire to understand his place in the world, and more importantly, his relationship to his God.

> For many years, in my painting, I have concentrated on light and colours, which, here in Australia, are often so violent. They correspond well to the tormented time that I was going through when I didn't really know which road to take, and my family thought that I was wasting my time. It was a way of giving vent to my feelings … When I came out again into the open air, I began to appreciate in a new way the details of objects, over and above their colour and form, and I began a series of paintings inspired by the Psalms in the Bible[8].

This led him to explore the forms and growth patterns of flowers, leaves, birds, butterflies and insects. These elements of the natural world were depicted with precision and respect, for he felt that '… this was enough to convey my understanding of God'[9]. He reconstructed each element from the garden, through a process of observation mediated by past experience and memory, to create a highly charged flower or leaf that could stand for all flowers and all leaves. In these early pictures Zofrea suggests that the garden is the quintessential environment for humanity, a place of peaceful meditation in which harmony and order reign. It is also notable within his personal symbology as the domain of his father and it is within this context that it is sometimes introduced into his reading of the Psalms. Zofrea's personal history intertwines with the narratives he recounts with such fluidity that the two often enmesh and in this case the image of God the gardener and his own father, tending his blooms, is used to suggest the larger family of the Christian church.

If the garden is the natural environment for humanity, the fabricated world of closed rooms and theatrical stages is the site of the fall. This notion is continually played out in the images of bordellos and crowded rooms where the baser aspects of human behaviour indicate the schism that occurs to separate individuals from their roots in the natural world. It is a rupture which can only be healed in heaven and, not surprisingly, heaven is invariably depicted as yet another garden. Final unity and harmony is given concrete form in the heavy, earth bound figures who roll in the grass and celebrate the pleasures of communion with nature and God. At a time when the deaths of his mother and his artistic mentor Henry Justelius had highlighted the sacredness of life and his own illness had reinforced its transitory nature, he began to explore this concept of heaven.

Beginning with *Psalm 3*, in which he places himself in a heavenly garden surrounded by young girls offering succour, he describes it a bountiful and harmonious place where those rewarded for their faith find peace and pleasure. There is little of the punitive aspects of the Judaeo-Christian tradition in Zofrea's work and these images of heaven are a good example of the positive messages he derives from the Psalms. Even when several of the texts contain descriptions of the terrible things that will befall the wicked or the weak, he identifies with the reassuring images of God's promise of final peace as the subject for his meditations. The death of his mother and his projection of her acceptance into heaven was an important factor in developing these images and accounts for the recurrence of this imagery in the early *Psalms*. It also explains his resort to an intensely awkward realisation of forms that has parallels with the work of naive artists like Henri Rousseau. The figures have a weight that is not only physically but also emotionally convincing as they caress and hold each other.

Stanley Spencer was another important model for the early *Psalms* and his wilful distortions of the human figure into painfully awkward gestures carries an intensity and conviction that Zofrea adopted in his paintings of heaven. He was concerned to give the figures a material density that set them apart as 'real' and tangible. Paradoxically the recourse to physicality is employed as a way of describing the world of the spirit. His heaven is not a vaporous, ethereal world but a solid and tangible reality. Just as Dante and the artists of the early Renaissance made heaven and hell visible, so Zofrea brings the spiritual into contact with the everyday by establishing its credentials for those on earth. One important aspect of this 'ever-present' heaven is the role of sensuality and sexuality. In heaven everyone is young and their gyrating, swirling sense of adoration and celebration is just another form of social intercourse. Men and women find succour in each others' company and the pleasures of 'a roll in the grass' are transposed into heaven as the just deserts of the faithful. The culmination of these pictures is the massive *Psalm 24 — In Heaven*, a celebration of his mother's entry into heaven. On her arrival she is hugged by her father and reunited with the children she lost in her lifetime. It is the clarity of the artist's vision that convinces us of this union between humanity and the forces of nature. Each flower is so precisely drawn and rendered, each petal and blade of grass so sharply outlined that we are encouraged to acknowledge the metaphysical component as an extension of the everyday world.

This absolute clarity and the artist's conviction that the most significant spiritual events are interwoven into the fabric of our lives is another expression of his 'innocent vision'. Of course he is not naive, his sophistication as an artist is evident in the ways in which he borrows, where necessary, from the early Renaissance, Rousseau or Spencer. The important consideration in his adoption of both the naive and the aware, informed position is the desire to imbue his vision with the quality of unaffected, childlike wonder.

BORGIA

CHILDHOOD IS A very special time for Salvatore Zofrea. It is a time inextricably associated with the small Calabrian village of Borgia were he was born and lived until the age of nine.

> When I look back on life in Borgia, I can see that my main sources of nourishment were my mother, the countryside, and the Church. My mother's loyalty, encouragement and friendship sustained me both as a child and also in later years when I used to work at labouring jobs by day and paint by night and at weekends; the Church and the countryside of Calabria repeatedly stunned me with their sensational pageants of colour[10].

This crucial early experience so deeply imbedded itself within his psyche that his *Psalms* are a conjunction of imagery derived from the ebb and flow of life in

Borgia, his religious experiences, the Bible, and his family. For this reason many of the paintings suggest a nostalgic past, preserved in memory:

> Our house was like all country houses, one large room, in fact a huge room of rammed earth divided by makeshift walls. In winter there was always a fair in the town. This was the pig season. All the families would kill their pig to prepare the salted meats for winter, and it was a great occasion for everybody. We made masks, we leapt and danced — in short, it was a great fair. In fact, just recently I have portrayed in one of my paintings a scene of people wearing grotesque masks which dates back to my memories of my childhood in Calabria [11].

There is a long tradition of artists setting Biblical events in a contemporary environment to suggest the continuing relevance of the lives of the Saints and Christ to the time in which they live. From the early Renaissance through to Breughel, Rembrandt, Spencer and Arthur Boyd the siting of the significant events of the Christian faith in contemporary Leyden, Cookham or Melbourne acts to deny time. As Roger Grainger explains when discussing the function of holy rite:

> Symbolic ritual is a structure for *presenting* — making past and future, near and far, fact and fantasy, *present* ... Whatever is immediate is present. Time, with its power to modify and limit, its power to *reduce*, has been banished. Within the symbol, past, present, and future may be juxtaposed as in a play, so that all is made to serve the meaning which inspires and precedes it, indeed meaning itself is all that reaches us. We become aware of an ideal truth, a truth which has been stripped of its time-scale, and with it of its contingent and particularised nature, and provided with a structure for happening here and now, and for including us in the immediate experience of things which demand,not our detached contemplation or our rational assessment, but our surrender and our participation [12].

Zofrea's art is a form of *representing* the images and experiences of his childhood and grafting them onto his experiences as an adult. The distanced, nostalgic past is made present, while retaining its qualities of purity and freshness, unhindered by the relentless drive of industrialisation and technology. People dance to a hand wound gramophone in rooms bare of televisions or chrome chairs. It is an experience to learn from, like the Bible, which although pertinent to our lives is couched in a language and set of customs that is unfamiliar. These elements assist us in accepting the 'ideal truth' of the Psalms because they are untainted, as the artist explains:

> Through the eyes of a child, the men and women of my small village were timeless people and their costume had a sort of volume and shape which grew out of an earthy simplicity. That's what stuck in my mind when I was able to recognise people and I think they really became the fixed models of my life [13].

In the ways in which Grainger suggests, the paintings in this series are structured to encourage our participation rather than offer themselves as the subject of detached contemplation or rational assessment. Zofrea calls upon the cinematic device of the flashback to further engage us in his narratives. These references to his past blur the distinction between past and present, bringing it into a vital relationship with contemporary events.

In *Psalm 17* he introduces an event that occurred in Borgia when he was three years old as the key to understanding the theme of deceit played out by the other characters in the painting. After agreeing to suckle the breast of a woman in the village, in return for a religious picture, he was rebuffed on completion of the task when the woman claimed she had lost the painting. This event is presented as a flashback within the larger narrative of seduction and deceit. It is the hub around

Photograph: Gordon Serfontein

which the theme of the painting revolves. He also frequently uses the 'present historic' tense in telling his stories as a way of further convincing us of the immediacy and relevance of his message. The past is described as a continuous present, as if told by a young child recalling wondrous events. In several of the *Psalms* the artist actually includes himself as a participant, looking out from the past to address us in the present. *Psalm 16*, for example, shows him in the costume of a page boy in Borgia, at his sister's wedding, recast as an observer of this scene of awakening sexuality. This direct contact with the viewer identifies him as the narrator of this tale, and in a very real sense he is; both as a child and as the adult artist constructing the painting.

Borgia is also the scene of the artist's earliest religious experiences and as such it remains the key influence in determining much of his religious imagery — in particular the conjunction between the Church and the circus, discussed in some detail later in this essay, and the sense of ritual. As he explains in the interview included in this volume:

> I would go down to the local creek and get bowls of clay and come back and do my little sculptures of each particular Saint or the Madonna. It was real to me as it was for the grown up people in the streets. I would reenact the ceremony and ask my family to participate as I walked down the street with this little image. To me it was the full thing[14].

The religious parades and celebrations where always crowded events in which family and friends joined together to the accompanied of music and noise to celebrate significant religious events. This conjunction of family life with the life of the Church plays a crucial role in understanding the artist's picturing of the Psalms:

> As Zofrea talks about the saints, it becomes obvious that the mainspring of his art is indeed religion — not the timid, Anglo-Saxon, antiseptic, arms-length type, but the full blooded Italian belief that comes from the heart. 'About Christ and the after life — I believe it. I never question it'[15].

Farming communities plant and harvest according to the phases of the moon and as the lunar calendar also dictates Saint's days and Christian holidays, the daily experience of attending Mass or consulting the Bible becomes an integral part of life. A family meal, for example, is one of the most important events in any peasant community because it is not only linked to physical sustenance but it is also a moment of spiritual reflection when the food is dedicated to God. In these ways Borgia remains at the core of the series as the *locus in quo* of personal and Biblical narratives that intertwine in Zofrea's meditations on the themes he identifies in the Psalms.

IN PERSPECTIVE

THE ROLE OF Borgia and the importance of Zofrea's Italian heritage in generating the imagery of his paintings might suggest a marginal role for his work in the broad canvas of Australian art history, as the product of a 'migrant artist'. Without denying the significance of his documentation of the experiences of many migrants[16], such an assessment would be misguided for Salvatore Zofrea works within the wider traditions of Australian art and International art. In fact it is his exploration of personal themes through a complex amalgam of figurative sources that gives his work its contemporary significance.

Not withstanding this aspect of Zofrea's art, it is important to identify the role of Italian art and artists in contributing to the construction of Australian culture, for it does indicate another level of interaction that is important in understanding his work.

The Italian Renaissance constitutes what Lyotard would call the fundamental 'master narrative' of the Western artistic tradition and many Australian artists from the early days of settlement have returned to that well-spring as a way of establishing contact with the past. This was seen as a profoundly conservative exercise earlier in the century, however, more recently the alignment with the iconography and formal qualities of Renaissance art has welcomed back an audience previously eschewed by the domination of Modernist ideology[17].

All white Australian artists are migrants and each to some degree carries that 'master narrative' with them, but for first and second generation Italian/Australian artists the Renaissance is not only a significant feature of their artistic culture they also carry it with them as the historical memory inherited from their parents[18].

The balance they fabricate between these notions of culture and their experiences of living in Australia is the key to establishing any sense of Australian identity.

In the case of Salvatore Zofrea, the early Renaissance is a crucial experience, not only because he is able to situate himself within the long tradition of Italian art, but also because the iconography of the Renaissance is designed to construct complex narratives that interweave personal histories with Biblical or pagan stories, historical events and the occurrences of everyday life. It is therefore ideally suited to his project of developing a commentary on the Psalms.

An important consideration when discussing the development of landscape painting in Australian is an assessment of the impact of the European tradition of visualising the land. As this tradition was greatly influenced by Italian art during the late seventeenth century, when Australia was first explored by Europeans, it forms another direct line in the Italian connection.

The first Italian artists to depict Australia were members of a Spanish expedition in 1793, Ferdinando Brambilla and Giovanni Ravenet, who produced paintings of the exotic native flora and fauna[19]. They were followed by several convict artists of Italian extraction, notably Charles Constantini. More importantly, any artist who did record the new landscape could not escape the contemporary dominance of the Roman School of landscape painting personified by the French painter Claude Lorraine, who lived much of his life in Rome. It was the impact of this classical landscape tradition that was fundamental in shaping the image of Australia presented by Thomas Watling, John Glover, Conrad Martens, W.C. Piguenit and Eugene von Guérard.

From the nineteenth century until well into the twentieth century there were also many images of a Southern Arcadia, developed in part from its source in Classical art and from Italian painting in particular. Tom Roberts, Arthur Streeton, Charles Conder and Sydney Long were some of the most prominent artists who expounded upon this myth and it is this version of the Australian landscape that is chosen by Salvatore Zofrea as the setting for his *Psalms*. The cultivated hills around Kurrajong and the sweeping vistas of the Hawkesbury River recall the landscape of his native Calabria and have the same stamp of human habitation. It is a landscape that reflects the passage of white Australians and contains their history and because it is charged with something of the same intensity of European landscape painting it strikes a cord with the artist.

By the late years of the nineteenth century, Australian artists were financially secure enough to travel and like thousands of their European colleagues they chose to follow the lead set by Doctor Johnson in 1776:

> A man who had not been to Italy is always conscious of an inferiority, from his not having seen what it is expected a man should see. The grand object of all travelling is to see the shores of the Mediterranean [20].

From that period until the present day the number of Australian artists who have made a pilgrimage to Italy and painted Italian subjects, includes many of Australia's best known artists; such as Arthur Streeton, Tom Roberts, Sidney Nolan, Lloyd Rees, Colin Lanceley and Brett Whiteley. Indeed the lure of Italy has been so powerful that it has led many Australians to settle permanently or for considerable periods of time in the Tuscan hills or amidst the bustle of Rome. Adelaide Ironside was one of the first and even today artists like Arthur Boyd, Justin O'Brien, Jeffrey Smart, Ken Whisson and Keith Looby live in Italy or maintain houses there. As Justin O'Brien explains:

> That's what I stay here for. I feel when I walk here that I'm standing on my heritage. When I'm in Australia I don't feel like that at all. Even though it's the oldest continent, to me it's new [21].

Interestingly this latter day pilgrimage to Italy has often been sponsored by big business (an example is the now defunct Flotto-Lauro Prize and the Mandorla Prize for religious art) and more recently by the Australian Government through their three studios (Paretaio, Besozzo and the Verdaccio studio). Whether these artists are in search of cultural roots, exotic experiences or just a sympathetic environment in which to work is arguable, but the number of pilgrims to the shrine and their enthusiasm, expressed in their work on returning to Australia, indicates an umbilical relationship that has sustained many generations [22].

For first and second generation Italian/Australian artists the trip to Italy represents a more complex dialectic conflict between their inherited culture and their experiences of living and working as an artist in Australia.

> I felt very strongly the alienation from Australia as a painter because my work didn't relate to the Australian way of life or the landscape. Even my grouping of people was Italian ... Finally last Christmas I got there. My heart just leapt when I touched Italian soil. As soon as I saw Giotto and Piero della Francesca I knew where I belonged [23].

Zofrea made his first trip to Europe in 1972 and although he didn't get to Italy he saw many masterpieces of the Italian Renaissance, including two of Uccello's three versions of the battle of San Romano. Then in 1982 he travelled to Calabria, Rome and Tuscany to renew contact with his Italian family and to do research for a series of paintings on the lives of St Francis and St Claire. More importantly he rediscovered the painters of the early Renaissance:

> ... I realised that by coming to Italy, by being on Italian soil with access to its vast store of treasure (architecture, painting, the lot) and seeing the works of Fra Angelico, Giotto and Piero della Francesca 'in the flesh' I could now relinquish the particular (my family and childhood memories) for the general. Seeing the works that combined simplicity of form with tremendous attention to detail, strengthened me for my future work [24].

During 1986 he returned again on a Churchill Fellowship to study Fresco with Leonetto Tintori and made contact with Uccello's third version of the battle of San Romano in the Uffici. The street life of Florence and images of small villages and holiday resorts also provided the source material for a number of paintings on his return.

For Zofrea these experiences were a confirmation of his Italian heritage and its relevance to his work. The conflict was resolved by emphasising his Italianness and assimilating it with his experiences of being a migrant in a nation of migrants. Just as several contemporary artists such as Tony Clark and Geoff Lowe have grafted their experience of the Renaissance through photographic reproductions onto their art as one way of establishing their roots in this country, so Zofrea has merged his complex relationship to Italian art with his practice as an Australian artist.

In seeking to place Salvatore Zofrea within the broad spectrum of Australian art the names of Justin O'Brien and Arthur Boyd come to mind. Both derive sustenance from the long tradition of Italian and European painting, they live and maintain homes in Italy and both illustrate Biblical narratives using their personal environments as the site for these stories. Nevertheless, there is not a great deal of similarity between their treatment of these narratives and the highly personalised interweaving of the spiritual and the everyday found in Zofrea's *Psalms*. However deeply felt, they describe the distanced gaze of the detached observer. Zofrea's vision is a struggle with his beliefs, played out in the images of his family, his environment and his knowledge of art history. It is a response reflected in Patrick White's autobiography *Flaws in the Glass*:

> What do I believe? I am accused of not making it explicit. How to be explicit about a grandeur too overwhelming to express, a daily wrestling match with an opponent whose limbs never become material, a struggle from which the sweat and blood are scattered on the pages of anything the serious writer writes? A belief contained less in what is said than in the silences. In patterns on water. A gust of wind. A flower opening[25].

Zofrea is not unique in contemporary Australian art; there are numerous artists exploring the possibilities of large scale narrative painting — Bernard Sachs, Jon Cattapan, Tom Alberts, Bernard Ollis, Pat Hoffie and the recent works of Fred Cress to name a few. What singles his work out is the fusion of the personal with the spiritual, the private with the universal.

Outside Australia there are more direct comparisons to be drawn, in particular with the work of Max Beckmann and Fernand Leger. Beckmann's desire to make pictures that had meaning and served some purpose was paramount in his artistic credo, as Friedhelm Fischer points out in his monograph on the artist:

> Beckmann was not interested in problems of form. In his view the problems that mattered were those of the world itself, and they could not be solved by commenting on the art of painting itself ... to do so was to confuse the end with the means[26].

Salvatore Zofrea shares this belief in the primacy of the message and the necessity to shape the means to fit the end. In doing so, he has borrowed frequently from the stylistic solutions of other artists like Beckmann, Leger and other figurative painters. However, the major similarity between Beckmann and all the others artists who have provided artistic inspiration to Zofrea, is their commitment to releasing the mystery contained within the simplest, most commonplace of objects. As Fischer in his commentary on Beckmann explains, this entails a commitment to figuration:

> In the preface to a catalogue of 1917 he (Beckmann) sums up his programme in three

demands: the artist must be a child of his age, he must be naturalistic towards his own
self and objective as regards his 'inner vision' ... Far from excluding each other, the
commitment of a visionary and the ruthless clairvoyance of an observer must work
together for a single end. To put it another way, the everyday world of encrusted material things will not give up its secrets but will only become more ghostlike, as long as
people and objects are withdrawn from the scope of artistic reflection and replaced by
abstractions[27].

The 'commitment of a visionary and the ruthless clairvoyance of an observer'
succinctly defines the parameters of Zofrea's ambitions as a painter. He, too, is
almost anachronistically iconographic or symbolist in his treatment of imagery and
at the same time radically original in his emotional response to the great truths and
questions of contemporary life. When combined with the heroic perspective of
Leger, objects in his paintings take on a new significance:

Balzac, Dostoevsky are two whom I always reread with the same fascination. They have
a sense of the 'close up' ... moving toward *personification through enlarged detail*, the indi-
vidualisation of the fragment where the drama begins, is set, and stirs. The object by
itself is capable of becoming something absolute, moving and dramatic.[28]

The combination of all of these small events constructs a complex narrative
that is both universally significant and highly personal. As Leger said 'A nose, an
eye, a foot, a hand or a jacket button becomes a precise reality'[29]. While these early
Modernist masters were vital in establishing the formal and conceptual framework
of Zofrea's art, the worldwide return to figuration in the early eighties provided an
added impetus to his explorations.

The Italian art critic Achille Bonito Oliva has pointed out the remarkable
affinity between Mannerist art of the late Renaissance and the art of the eighties.
After the almost divine perfection of the Renaissance many artists rebelled by
adopting excessive distortions, parodic dramatisations, highly artificial lighting,
outrageous eroticism and brilliantly conceived illusions. Similarly, in the face of
Minimal Art, Conceptual Art and austere International Modernist architecture,
artists from Germany and Italy (in particular but in effect all over Europe and the
Western World) began to emphasise:

... what is charming, odd, risque, they mobilise the myths of the past, unite the incom-
patible ... Outwardly of course, the special character of Mannerist painting is totally different. Today's works of art do not have anything precious about them, nor are they particularly spiritual or programmatic. They are less desperate and more playful and
rambling. Nevertheless, there are some striking parallels: the artist's assertion of his
ego, his emphasis on extreme subjectivity, the physiological element and an obsession
with the human body ... the lack of homogeneity of the world they paint, the multiple
fragmentation of the painting's structure, their tendency to narrate, and the unusual
choice of colour[30].

The works of Cucchi, Chia, Clemente and Paladino are essays in self-discovery that interweave imagery borrowed from the Renaissance, early Modernism
and the religious and cosmological visions of eastern, western and tribal art. They
appeal to the emotions and the intellect by using the traditional techniques of oil
painting, fresco, mosaics, bronze casting and drawing as a field within which to
explore their egos in a game about art and life.

While a good deal of the irony and parodic intention of these artists lies outside Zofrea's programme their approach to subjectivity as a structuring device for
their art, their interest in plundering the visual storehouse of world art as source
material and the tangible sense of mystery they are able to weave around the
objects and places they describe, provides an international context for his *Psalms*.

Even accepting these contemporary comparisons, though, it is too simplistic to suggest that Salvatore Zofrea is an Australian member of the *Trans-avant garde*. In fact it is far from the mark because the other essential element of his work is the link to the decorative traditions of folk art and the *quattrocento*. He uses these sources as a means of giving form to his meditations on Christianity and its responses to the great questions of existence. This quiet, self-contained approach is outside the contrived awkwardness and ironical stance of these contemporary artists.

While his exploration of personal themes is conducted through a complex amalgam of figurative sources that mine the mystery and surprise in what Rimbaud described as 'that other world, this one', another important influence reinforces his separation from their work.

THE SPECIAL CASE OF STANLEY SPENCER

THE AFFINITY WITH Spencer is evident in the first body of works produced within the series of paintings of the Psalms. Zofrea was drawn to the deep religious commitment and the local focus that sustained Spencer throughout his life, his obsessive search for detail and structure and the vein of sensuality and sexuality that run just beneath the surface of his paintings. These are all elements that have a parallel in Zofrea's approach to the pictures preceding the *Psalms* (*The Child Buddha in the Garden* and *Waiting for the Barbarians*).

Nevertheless, the early *Psalms* are even more indebted to Spencer in their adoption of the inflated, almost pneumatic, figures, the swirling patterns that wrap around human forms and the landscape, and the location of Biblical narratives and events in a very personal, localised space. As the artist explains:

> The only person I came back to was Stanley Spencer. He was the only painter who came close to my method of using everyday experiences because he also used his family and showed people as they were, with their big, fat, wobbly legs. He used them to bring out the whole crescendo of emotion he portrayed and I could see a lot of my own spirit in his work[31].

While Zofrea goes on to point out the link to Giotto and the painters of the *quattrocento* which establishes this connection as an extension of his programme as an artist, other commentators have seen the strength of this influence as a difficulty when approaching the early *Psalms*. According to Terry Smith:

> While the sincerity of these and other works is beyond doubt, Zofrea's artistic program has, for me, been compromised by its profound indebtedness to the great English academic eccentric, Stanley Spencer.
>
> Spencer's Cookham, Berkshire, was filled with Christ's presence long before Zofrea saw the parallel in his own birthplace, Borgia in Calabria ... Zofrea drew so heavily on Spencer in the mid-1970s that it is hard to tell them apart. The same blimp-like figures convey ecstasy beyond earthly beauty, and wear the same sackcloth. Landscapes have the same close-up exactitude, as in *Crows Nest Annunciation*, 1981[32].

The influence is undoubted and acknowledged by the artist, yet while Smith's criticism is pertinent an examination of the early *Psalms* indicates how much Zofrea has plumbed from his artistic mentor. It is not only the stylistic borrowings that take root and flower in more complex and surprising forms in the later paintings, what is more significant is an attitudinal approach to the content that helped to shape his reading of the Psalms. Like Spencer he is attracted to the idea of Christianity (in his case Catholicism) as an external moral authority even though he is wary of actually submitting to it[33].

Zofrea associates Christianity with realism. Consequently the veracity of the smallest detail leads him to examine the world through the magnifying glass of his own experiences and to give these details the weight of his convictions. The concrete density of his images is derived from Spencer, but it is more a response to his belief in the presence of the spiritual in the objects of everyday life. The clarity with which these details are rendered replicates the unadulterated vision of childhood; a sense of the absolute certainty of the believer. This vision, coloured as it is by Spencer's pervasive image of sexuality, his belief in the sanctity of human life, and his visionary gift is important because it gives form to those same aspirations in Zofrea's work. Later paintings show how he was able to find his own solutions to those problems of resolution, but initially it was Spencer who acted as the primary model for this exploration of his religious convictions.

TRIALS AND REDEMPTION

THE PSALMS GREW out of physical suffering so it is not surprising that the central theme Zofrea extracts from many of the Psalms is the image of the trial. Life is described as a series of trials through which each individual must pass before receiving their final salvation in heaven. In the same way that Spencer saw the spiritual in the everyday and was able to acknowledge life as a religious activity, so Zofrea explores these ideas in the events of his life and through the experiences of his family and friends.

A significant difference however, is the more punitive aspect of Zofrea's Catholicism. Whereas Spencer rarely resorts to suffering, preferring to give visual form to adoration, celebration and atonement (choosing to ignore Christ's suffering on the cross as the traditional model for atonement)[34], Zofrea depicts suffering, deceit, retribution, vengeance and the gamut of psychological and physical trials as the status quo for human beings.

Photograph: Gordon Serfontein

The dance of life (or death) is a recurring theme that introduces sexuality as a major combative field for humanity. In numerous paintings the conflict between men and women is seen as a trial that must be encountered, whatever the consequences — almost always dire. Sexuality is a force that is present in all Zofrea's paintings and its relation to his conception of religion is a complex amalgam of grass roots Catholicism and late twentieth century libertarianism. Sex is seen as the natural right of human beings and the source of their greatest pleasure, as well as their nadir. While the home may be the shrine of the first, the bordello is seen as the setting for men and women's degradation.

Women are generally divided into two well known categories, the whore and the madonna, and by siting many of the pictures in a brothel Zofrea aligns sexuality with illicit barter in which neither the girl nor the client are entirely free of guilt. Most often however, it is the men who are held responsible for the degradation this engenders, as in *Psalm 14 — Que Dice Donna Dice Donna*, but women are also accused of collusion in this dangerous game. They are sometimes shown as vain creatures staring into mirrors, preparing themselves to ensnare men.

The complexity of his depiction can be assessed by his comparison between a defiled woman and Christ Forsaken on the Cross in *Psalm 22*. In contrast another woman is shown summoning up the horned beast of lust in *Psalm 29 — Il Sogno*.

Woman is at once the clairvoyant innocent, as in *Psalm 26 (Loren)* and the two headed, bare breasted, sharp taloned eagle tearing into the prostrate young man's flesh, in *Psalm 42*.

If the artist's position on the woman's role is ambivalent he has an equally complex image of male sexuality that covers the gamut from rampant centaur to pathetic victim. The mind/body split, personified in the physical form of the centaur in *Psalm 45* and *48*, is the key to understanding the tensions that underlie the game of love for Zofrea. In his game plan men are driven by their sexual desire and terrified by its power. The coarse and irrational forces represented by the centaur are unleashed by sexual desire in a Dionysian orgy that the righteous and rational side of his personality cannot control. In horror he must sit to one side and watch as the libido takes over. As both aggressor and victim the man is afflicted with his own sexuality from puberty to old age. As a young boy, pure and innocent, he is free from the trial of his sexuality, but he does not retain that freedom again until he finds final redemption in heaven. Only then does sex become the uncomplicated, pleasurable act he dreams of.

The one exception is the exuberant celebration of human intimacy in *Psalm 30 — Rosa*. It is a riot of physicality and sensuality. The thick fleshy thighs of Rosa's beau and her own ample limbs are painted with relish and the none too delicate contact between the couple seems to resound through the picture.

Throughout the *Psalms* card players are often juxtaposed against lovers to contrast the familiarity of mates with the joys and dangers of sexuality and to emphasise the notion that life is a game in which each move has a consequence. Of course, it also suggests that life is a gamble and raises the possibility of stacked decks, bad hands and cheating. The imagery of card playing is linked to men, and in particular to the artist's father and family, so while it retains the associations with deceit and insubstantiality (the house of cards) that are imbedded within our language, it also becomes a symbolic connection to the trials associated with masculinity.

If sexuality in general and male sexuality in particular is seen as one of the most ensnaring trials for humanity, the death of his father and mother raised the all-encompassing notion of human existence as a trial. Of all the images of the trials of life, those associated with the busker the artist saw in the streets of Florence are the most perspicuous. The young busker putting his animals through their painful trials was a potent image that enabled the artist to accommodate his sense of disorientation and pain on the death of his father:

> It was painful and I realised how I could use these images in my depiction of the Psalms to show how we exploit life and exploit each other[35].

The cat on its swing, the goat with its ridiculous pom-pom and the caged bird represent humanity put though its trial of existence by a group of buskers and circus people. The lights that hang above the scene in many of the paintings from this series are a symbol of heaven or the prospect of heaven. Below is the temporal world of trial and punishment, of disorientation and pain, that is only made bearable by the promise of redemption. Associated with this theme is the image of a carousel and also a battle — to be specific, the battle of San Romano from Paulo Uccello's great fifteenth century cycle of three paintings.

If life is merely a series of hoops and trials it is not to be addressed resignedly.

Zofrea is contemptuous of those who pass through the flaming hoops without making some attempt to determine the course of their own lives. In *Psalm 32 — The Carousel* the central character breaks free from the repetitive gestures of the merry-go-round and sets his own course while those that remain are condemned to play out the game of war for all eternity. Zofrea believes that humanity must continue to search out the meaning of life by confronting these trials and the only release in his theology is that offered by an acceptance of God's final solution to the pain and suffering encountered throughout life. In heaven these questions are finally answered and, he suggests, it is the promise of that peace which drives us on.

CROWDED ROOMS

ZOFREA'S WORLD IS full of human beings all jostling together. Whether it be in the family home, a cafe, a bordello or heaven, in all but a few notable exceptions, the place is crowded. Being the last child in a large family might account for this vision of the world, however the artist has given this image special significance by adopting a claustrophobic space full of people as a major structuring device for his *Psalms*. Not only does it contain the drama, it is designed in such a way that it produces the tensions that explain the dynamic situations occurring within its walls.

The enclosed room, sealed off from outside and with no visible windows or doors for escape, is the venue for conflict. Most often crowded to overflowing with people and animals, the claustrophobia is palpable as each makes their own space by cutting themselves off from visual or physical contact with one another. Although swept up in the conflicts and pressures of life they seek anonymity or at least separateness.

It must be pointed out that although crowding is most often associated with personal drama and conflict, the compression of the picture plane is a useful device for engaging the viewer in the events depicted. In heaven or a bordello the weighty figures stand cheek by jowl within the confining space of the painting demanding our attention and the elimination of any visual escape assures our participation, just as much as it does theirs.

In many cases the rooms are painted at night when an internal lighted space is a retreat from the dangers associated with darkness. Paradoxically these rooms do not provide the warmth and protection we might assume, instead they are places where deceit, exploitation and indifference prevail. In *Psalm 17* the interior becomes a containing device for the totality of human experience and the pressure on the picture plane, created by the stifling overcrowding, draws us into these relationships as conspirators. Although it might appear on the surface as a large, happy family gathering, the internal tensions, the averted glances, the sleight of hand, overt provocation and innuendo suggest a very different reading.

In the later *Psalms* as the ambience becomes darker and more ominous, the space squeezes in on the figures with even greater force. The combined effect of these changes is to create a pressure cooker in which human emotion is kept at boiling point to involve the viewer in the events described. Only the timelessness of the painting acts as a safety valve to keep the drama under control.

Zofrea has developed this approach to picture making over the past few years as a way of exorcising his own devils and also as a means of drawing his audience into a closer relationship with the psychological tensions he depicts. His belief that great art can only emerge from significant physical and emotional experiences is extended into a theory of reception which is based on the ability of individuals to identify their own experiences in those represented in the painting. The Psalms operate as a trigger for the artist's introspective meditation on his life and through this act of self-discovery, the viewer is reconfirmed in their own beliefs through the veracity of those experiences. They can say 'I know what it's like for that to happen to me', explains Zofrea, and because of that connection they transcend the specific events depicted and expand them to embrace a universal truth about existence.

One of the most effective devices he employs to secure the involvement of the viewer is the structuring of the painting to concur with their physical reality and the adoption of a viewpoint that situates them in an intimate relationship with the people depicted in the painting. In *Psalm 5* we are constantly drawn back to the central figure because of the clever innovation of emphasising the gradual blurriness of peripheral vision. The mother figure is substantial and in sharp focus in the centre of our field of vision, her solid fleshy hand hovering three centimetres above her plate. However, as we move out from the centre each element becomes less and less distinct until the dark figure in the chair dissolves into a thin veil of stained colour. This creates a vortex that keeps drawing us back into the centre through a simulation of our modes of seeing.

How we see is of course a vital consideration, but the vantage point from where we see is no less critical in establishing our relationship with the events depicted. Viewpoint is a fundamental device in constructing a relationship with the viewer and in most of the *Psalms* an examination of the vantage point allotted to viewers can determine the type of response the artist seeks from his audience. An instructive comparison is offered by two early *Psalms*. In *Psalm 6* the artist places us into an intimate relationship with the old man in his garden by placing the viewer at his eye level as he silently contemplates the blooms in his garden. In other words the viewer is also on their knees sharing this moment of quiet contemplation. The everyday familiarity of this image suggests participation, however, there are events of a transcendental kind that preclude actual involvement. By adopting an all pervasive, 'Baroque' perspective in *Psalm 7*, he sets the viewer free to hover in space and move like a spectre through various rooms as a way of emphasising the other worldliness of the experience.

Within the crowded rooms more intimate vantage points are employed to locate us as participants. In *Psalm 14 — Que Dice Donna Dice Donna*, the artist places the viewer amongst the clients of the bordello by seating them at the eye level of the men on the red velvet settees. Clearly they are on another chair on the opposite side of the room. It is obvious from the organisation of this painting that the artist will not allow the viewer to be uninvolved.

Even in the one painting of the series that does not include a human figure the viewpoint from which the scene is observed suggests that the viewer is 'in' the room. This involvement is given added weight by the mobilisation of other sensory modes. Smell and sound in particular are Zofrean favourites. An early experience of joining in religious festivals in Borgia has given the artist potent models for this way of working and in this Psalm the sound of the wind and the smell of magnolias are invoked to draw us further and further into the implications of the scene described.

This range of possibilities is milked for all its potential so that either as detached observer, audience, participant or co-conspirator the viewer is in no doubt as to their relationship to the narrative unfolding in the painting.

CLOWNS, FOOTLIGHTS AND THE 'CLOSE-UP'

AFTER THE CROWDED room the circus or carnival is the favoured locale for Zofrea's setting of his *Psalms*.

In Borgia, Saint's days were the cause of much celebration, with visiting circuses or travelling fairs set up in the village. Consequently the conjunction of the fairground with the church, of entertainment and frivolity with deeply held beliefs, is now at the root of his narrative technique.

The associations with vanity and folly, with the image of the world as a mad-house, has a singular attraction to him because it allows a good deal of theatricality while remaining true to his experience. Max Beckmann employed the circus for similar reasons as Friedhelm Fischer explains:

> … since the late medieval *Ship of Fools* it was common to associate human folly in general with the grotesqueries of a carnival cortege. In the Baroque period this thought was extended into a parallel between the world and the comic stage: in the sight of God or eternity the petty doings of mankind, in fact the whole of human history, were no better that an idle farce. In the early twenties, Beckmann found this last comparison particularly appropriate. Indeed he went further that the Baroque satirists by taking as his target not only mankind but the director of the theatre himself: 'My pictures are a reproach to God for all he does wrong'[36].

Although Zofrea is more inclined to draw a parallel between the circus and humanity's trials rather than comment on God's perversity, the acknowledgment of the artifice of the stage, with its flimsy backcloth, bright unmodulated colour and straightforward presentation in a shallow space, opened up new avenues through which to explore his ideas on the superficiality of life and the transitory nature of our existence.

One theatrical device employed in many of the *Psalms* is the inclusion of a figure who seeks out eye contact with the viewer, either as an attempt to illicit our support or as a clear message that the reality of the painting is merely an extension of everyday reality. It is designed to shake the viewer from their role as distanced observer in much the same way that Brecht used his 'alienation effect' to shock his audience out of their secure indifference. The young boy in many of the *Psalms* (actually Zofrea as a page boy) fulfils this role brilliantly because his gaze is so ingenuous and appealing that to deny his entreaty would be callous. It is a clever device which enables the artist to address his audiences as both innocent observer and conjurer.

Another frequent tool in his paintings is the use of theatrical lighting to spot-light characters. Within those darkened, crowded rooms that appear so regularly throughout the series, individuals and groups are brought to our attention by the use of strong lighting, often emanating from off stage. The intensity that this theatrical presentation lends to an image heightens the drama and at the same time proscribes the viewer's response. After all, artifice is the stock and trade of the proscenium arch theatre and even if the actors rupture this secure distance occasionally through a more direct contact, viewers know the parameters of their involvement. As a consequence the artist can play with the conventions of the theatre to expound on his theme while simultaneously guiding our responses.

In the busker paintings Zofrea continues to explore these ideas while injecting the experiences of fairs and circus folk from his childhood. In his vision circus people and gypsies represent the duality of human existence through their masking of true feelings and in particular the clown suggests the dangerous and duplicitous side of humanity, always ready to play a trick. However, while the theatrical element is extremely important, these paintings exploit the devices of the cinema more frequently than those of the theatre. Firstly, they are bathed in a strong natural light that floods all the characters and the set, eliminating the strong shadows and intense spotlighting found in the theatre. More importantly he employs the viewpoint and framing associated with the cinema. It is even possible to identify camera shots in many of the paintings. In *Psalm 16* for example, he mimics a cinematic pan that carries us around the action, lingering on the faces, the bodies and the reactions of each character. He then makes use of the mid-shot and close-up to draw us deeper into their world.

Finally the connection with the cinema is confirmed by the artist's appropriation of certain stills from films by his favourite directors. For example, the two men shaking hands in *Psalm 22* are borrowed from the film *The War Lord* and several of Fellini's films have provided either direct sources or inspiration. *Psalm 38* is indirectly inspired by the mood of many of Fellini's films in which characters find themselves in desolate summer resorts walking along the beach in the early hours of the morning or sitting in a cafe whose bamboo blinds crackle in the wind.

This connection with Italian film directors is not so surprising because several shared a similar background and some of the same early experiences as Zofrea. Like him they now use memories of childhood, religion, village life and their family as part of their films so when their images strike a chord he has no compunction in using them.

The pervasive influence of the methodology of film making also makes a significant contribution to his narrative techniques. While the dramatically lit *tableau vivant* offers many possibilities for developing a story line, the all encompassing flow of the cinema and the possibility of merging past, present and future through flash-backs and flash-forwards suggests others that expand the artist's vocabulary. In the busker paintings it is this cinematic narrative that takes precedence.

The circus, merry-go-rounds, the theatre, the performance of the busker and the cinema all have a special potency for the artist who sees them as a metaphor for the veneer of everyday life. The tormented souls putting on a happy face as they act out their parts *are* a microcosm of life, as Shakespeare explained in his inversion of the idea in *As You Like It*:

> All the world's a stage, And all the men and women merely players: They have their exits and their entrances: And one man in his time plays many parts, His acts being seven ages [37].

The world of the theatre and entertainment acts as a parallel universe providing a commentary on our everyday lives. By adopting many of the same devices and motives Zofrea's *Psalms* take on a similar role.

REVELATIONS

SALVATORE ZOFREA BEGAN painting the *Psalms* as a celebration of life and of his

Photograph: Willie Mobbs

rediscovery of Christianity. At a time of great personal suffering he sought solace in the beliefs of his childhood and on recovery he undertook to fulfil his promise to paint all 150 *Psalms*. Then as other tragedies struck during the completion of his first fifty meditations on the *Psalms* he quite naturally included them as further illustrations of the central theme revealed through his reading of the *Psalms* — trials and redemption.

Consequently this remarkable project is neither a theological analysis of the Psalms nor an illustration of Catholic dogma, it is a personal document that explores the great questions of human existence within the framework of one life.

Despite this highly individualised reading of the text it would be wrong to see Zofrea's Psalms as an idiosyncratic visual narrative which precludes the viewer. As we have seen the artist is determined to involve his audience; indeed he is not averse to proselytising and the insistent message that salvation awaits those who turn to Christ is delivered with all the energy and vehement entreaty one normally associates with an evangelist. Yet within this core of belief there is a multitude of conflicting ideas, confusions and frustrations. Salvatore Zofrea often turns to the visions of his childhood in search of absolute clarity, but like any intelligent human being living in the late twentieth century he acknowledges the inherent impossibility of achieving that state of perfect clarity.

Faced with the uncertainty and ambiguity of his own life he has developed a theology in which that way of knowing is moved outside the temporal domain and offered as the promised redemption from human suffering. In heaven all will be revealed and in this revelation humanity will find peace.

NOTES:

1. See Stephanie Claire's chapter in *Salvatore Zofrea* Hale & Iremonger, Sydney, 1983 for a more detailed description of the artist's early life in Borgia.
2. See Anna Waldmann's chapter in *Salvatore Zofrea*, 1983, for a comprehensive assessment of the artist's early career.
3. Daniel Thomas, *Sunday Telegraph*, 9 February, 1969, p.73.
4. Elwyn Lynn, 'Materialising images of concrete irrationality', *The Bulletin*, 8 February, 1969.
5. Alan McCulloch, 'Distilled wine from the world of pop', Melbourne *Herald*, October, 1972.
6. Eneide Mignacca, 'Geographical and chronological misfit', *Nation Review*, 7–13 June, 1974, p.6.
7. See Peter Fuller's analysis of Nolan's desert landscapes of the late 40's and 50's in *The Australian Scapegoat*, University of Western Australia Press, 1986.
8. C.B.M. 'Personale di Salvatore Zofrea il "Pittore dei Salmi"', *La Fiamma*, 9 August, 1976, p.11. (Translated by Jody Fitzhardinge)
9. Claire & Waldmann, op. cit., p.44.
10. Claire & Waldmann, ibid., p.18.
11. '15.ma personale di Salvatore Zofrea', *Il Globo — Sydney*, 7 August 1976, p.1.
12. Roger Grainger, *The Language of the Rite*, Darton, Longman & Todd, London, 1974, p.110.

13. Interview with Salvatore Zofrea, 12 February 1990, printed in this volume.

14. Ibid.

15. Sandra McGrath 'Psalm like it hot and fleshy', *The Australian*, 31 October, 1983, p.10.

16. Many of the artist's works describe the experiences of his family when they arrived in Australia, in particular the *Odyssey*, a series of woodcuts that depicts major migration and life cycle milestones, shown at the Macquarie Gallery in March 1990.

17. See, Naomi Cass's essay in *Renaissance References in Australian Art*, University Gallery, University of Melbourne, 1985.

18. See Marco Marcon's essay in *Memory and Identity*, Perth Institute of Contemporary Art, 1989.

19. For details of the early artists of Italian origin who worked in Australia see *Buongiorno Australia: Our Italian Heritage*, Robert Pascoe, Greenhouse Publications, Melbourne, 1987.

20. *The Oxford Dictionary of Quotations*, Oxford University Press, third edition with corrections, 1986, p.277.

21. Interview with the author, Rome, June 1988.

22. Ted Snell, 'The Australian Italian Connection', *Memory and Identity*, Perth Institute of Contemporary Art, 1989.

23. Sandra McGrath, Ibid.

24. Claire, Ibid, p.68.

25. Patrick White *Flaws in the Glass*, Jonathan Cape, London, 1981, p.70.

26. Friedhelm W Fischer *Max Beckmann*, Phaidon, London, 1973, p.6.

27. Ibid, p.23.

28. Fernand Leger 'Propos d'artistes' 1925, *Twentieth Century Art Theory*, Richard Hertz & Norman Klein, Prentice Hall, New Jersey, 1990, p.55.

29. John Russell, *The Meanings of Modern Art*, Thames and Hudson, London, 1981, p.257.

30. Klaus Honnef, *Contemporary Art*, Taschen, W Germany, 1988, p.101.

31. Interview with Salvatore Zofrea, 12 February 1990.

32. Terry Smith, 'From pole to pole in pursuit of faith', *Times on Sunday*, 13 December 1987, p.30.

33. See Andrew Causey's essay 'Stanley Spencer and the art of his time', in *Stanley Spencer RA*, Royal Academy of Art in association with Weidenfeld and Nicolson, London, 1980, for a comprehensive study of Spencer's work.

34. Ibid, p.24.

35. Interview with Salvatore Zofrea, 12 February 1990.

36. Op. cit, Fischer, p.25.

37. William Shakespeare, *The Complete Works of William Shakespeare*, Spring Books, London, 1976, p.218.

The First 50 Psalms

Psalm 1

Oil on canvas, 101.6 x 127.1 cm., 1976

'And he shall be like a tree...' Verse 3

While recovering from his first bout of illness Zofrea began his series on the theme of the Psalms with an image of God the gardener, tending his flowers in a private garden. Drawn from *Verse 3*, in which those who follow the word of God are likened to fruitful trees planted by a river, he constructed an image of a benign old man carefully checking the blooms in his lush garden. This paradise has been planned by the gardener to achieve the best results and consequently it is separated from the ungodly who, we are told in *Verse 5*, cannot stand '... in congregation with the righteous'.

The image of the gardener at peace with the universe has a particular poignancy for Zofrea whose father, a dedicated gardener, was the model for the painting. This link to family life is a recurrent theme in many of the paintings and it is appropriate that this analogy to the larger family of the Christian church is introduced at the beginning of his meditation on the Psalms.

Gardens recur in his work as the setting for solitary communion and social activity from an early stage, and in 1974 he employed a particularly bountiful garden as a metaphor for his search for God. *The Child Buddha in the Garden* was one of the first of a group of pictures that sought an inner truth through an analytical study of Nature rather than a physically responsive application of paint.

After working in an expressionist mode for more than a decade his desire to understand his place in the world, and most importantly his relationship to his God, led him to explore the forms and growth patterns of flowers, leaves, birds, butterflies and insects. These elements of the natural world were depicted with precision and respect for he felt that '... this was enough to convey my understanding of God'[1].

In the long tradition of imagery depicting a natural harmony, epitomised by the American naive painter Edward Hicks' *The Peaceable Kingdom*, Zofrea's *Buddha* exists in a simplified space in which the decorative forms of plants, birds and leaves interlock with preordained clarity. Each element is reconstructed from a process of observation mediated by past experience and memory to create a highly charged flower or leaf that demands our inspection. His interest in the elements of the natural world is not conditional on the fall of light or the atmosphere that surrounds them, so he is able to gather them together and set up dramatic incidents rather than purely visual experiences. This invocation of Blake's famous dictum 'To see a World in a Grain of Sand, And A Heaven in a Wild Flower'[2] carries over into the Psalms where the artist asks us to join with the gardener in meditating on each bloom — rather like saying a Rosary — as a stay against fear and a solace in the bounty of the earth.

1. *Salvatore Zofrea*, Stephanie Clare and Anna Waldmann, Hale & Iremonger, Sydney, 1983. p 44.
2. *Auguries of Innocence*, William Blake.

PSALM 2

Oil on canvas, 127.1 x 152.5 cm., 1976

'WHY DO THE HEATHEN RAGE, AND THE PEOPLE IMAGINE A VAIN THING.' Verse 1

If the garden is the place where peace and harmony reign, the enclosed room, sealed off from outside and with no visible windows or doors for escape, is the venue for conflict in many of Zofrea's paintings of the Psalms. Often crowded to overflowing with people and animals the claustrophobia is palpable as each makes their own space by cutting themselves off from visual or physical contact with one another. Why do they wait in fear, is it because they cannot hide from the wrath of God?

Vengeance and retribution are continuing themes throughout the Psalms and for Zofrea this is transposed into a psychological terror that pervades the room. Those that turn against God for their own ends will suffer just as the people in this room await punishment for their vanity, their stupidity or their desire for power. It is a telling image that powerfully evokes the terror of waiting.

Like so many of his paintings the setting for this drama is a reconstruction of his family home in Borgia, Calabria where animals, children and adults were swept up by the conflicts and pressures of family life. The memories of this experience have coloured his life because Zofrea was only a child when the family left Borgia and so the perspective of a child infuses this vision.

Consequently, his images of that experience have remained fixed in his childhood as a time capsule of the 1950s. This period setting creates a distanced nostalgia which situates the narrative outside our experience. It is something to learn from, like the Bible, which although pertinent to our lives is couched in a language and set of customs that is unfamiliar.

Although there are no direct sources other than his Calabrian memories the use of iconography and the visual weight of the figures derive from his interest in *quattrocento* Italian painting. The open book can be read as the search for wisdom, also evoked by the owl who sees in the night (the night of the human mind), while the pig is an image of gluttony, greed and stress. The monkey grasps the dove of freedom and each adult in the room hides their eyes. Only the innocent child, playing with his caged bird, shows no sign of anxiety.

On a formal level the shallow space of the room is reminiscent of Giotto and the solid figures who crowd this stage have the weight of his characters. This restricted space not only pushes the central figures out into contact with the viewers it draws us in to confront the narrative. Salvatore Zofrea acknowledges that all of the Psalms can be read as a form of self-portraiture so it is not unreasonable to interpret this image as his search for inner peace in the face of humanity's frailties and foibles. It is he who sits scanning the book of wisdom for the solution.

PSALM 3

Oil on canvas, 122 x 152.5 cm., 1976

'BUT THOU, O LORD, ART A SHIELD FOR ME: MY GLORY, AND THE LIFTER UP OF MINE HEAD.' Verse 3

After his illness Zofrea sought nurture in his painting. At a time when the deaths of his mother and his artistic mentor Henry Justelius had highlighted the sacredness of life and his own illness reinforced its transitory nature he took on the Psalms as a personal doctrine. Placing himself at the centre of the painting, surrounded by flowers and young girls offering succour, he was seeking the support of the scriptures through painting. 'I laid me down and slept: I awakened; for the Lord sustained me' (*Verse 5*).

These are not religious pictures in the traditional sense of illustrating Church dogma because the artist places the sacred within a lay domain to allow for a greater personal involvement from the viewer. The blunt edge of the commonplace is employed as a means of installing the viewer within the picture and allowing their own experiences to resonate with the ideas expressed. To facilitate this Zofrea invokes our sense of smell or hearing. Sounds and smells are often integral elements within his paintings and in this work the heavy, intoxicating scent of the magnolias and jasmine surrounding the central figure induces sleep.

We also feel the weight of the central characters whose substantial presence crowds the picture. In all the early Psalms the oversized figures draw us into the painting by suggesting a close focus and the dramatic foreshortenings and high or low viewpoints are calculated to involve us in the unfolding drama. The virtual denial of deep space also contributes to this end.

Technically this painting is remarkable for the interplay between flat pattern and volume which relates the inflated figures to the field by interlocking their outlines together, as if it were a jig-saw puzzle. Each form seems set by its rigid outline and yet the slow arabesques which wind through the composition weld them together into a harmonious unity. This is very appropriate because it highlights the fact that Zofrea's technical innovation is tied to the intellectual requirements he set for his pictures. The material density of his images grows out of his need to make manifest the 'truths' of the Psalm and to relate them to his own life. This compulsion can lead to an awkwardness when there is no model from memory of the bank of images the artist constantly accumulates but even then the urgency of the image is so convincing that it achieves an even greater intensity in the painting. The closest figure to us, about to offer a caress, is caught with her hand in an impossible position, yet we almost will it to make contact.

Involvement from his audience is paramount for Zofrea and even if it is not planned in the initial conception, his intuition takes over to assure our complicity in the action.

PSALM 4

Oil on canvas, 122 x 152.5 cm., 1976

'STAND IN AWE, AND SIN NOT: COMMUNE WITH YOUR OWN HEART UPON YOUR
BED, AND BE STILL ...' Verse 4

The bordello is a pervasive motif throughout Zofrea's work in general and in the
Psalms in particular. The prostitute is the most often portrayed woman in the art of
the first half of the twentieth century and the bordello the quintessential image of
debauchery. In this painting the working women are both in authority, and sub-
servient to men; they are objects to be desired and they are available. Nevertheless, for the implied 'male' viewer, there as a prospective client, the indifference of
these women to his presence must be very unsettling[1].

The duality of their role is certainly part of their attraction for artists, but as
John Berger has pointed out it is obviously hypocritical to castigate women for
their vanity in a painting that is clearly designed for the pleasure of the implied
male viewer[2]. In this Psalm Zofrea links the theme of vanity '... how *long* will ye
love vanity ...' (*Verse 2*) with a more elaborate narrative developed through the
introduction of the young girls playing outside in the sunshine and the tiny figure
of a client waiting for his partner. The lost innocence of the women is played off
against the possibility that the young girls may also end up in the bordello and the
tiny scale of the male figure suggests the indifference of the prostitutes while
simultaneously indicating the client's insecurity.

The atmosphere is charged with this sense of awkwardness which is given
concrete form in the image of the inverted cockatoo. This complex narrative is not
condemning because Zofrea has refused to take any high ground. His sympathy
for the women and their role is clear in his depiction of their dejected and awkward
poses, but the message that much is lost is made abundantly clear.

Originally written as a song and addressed 'To the Chief Musician upon
Nehiloth' the artist once again introduces music, in the form of an old gramophone, to animate the scene. This rhythmic pulsation runs through the composition as interweaving patterns, arabesques and silhouettes that flow over the fur-
nishings and figures to draw us into the action. Our involvement is not assured
however, because although the small Roman temple on the distant hill locates this
painting geographically in Italy, it is not set in the present. The gramophone and
heavily patterned brocades and wallpaper suggest a nostalgic past preserved in
memory and therefore outside our experience[3]. Zofrea is very comfortable in this
distanced world where his visual memory serves to define each object represented
with a material density that is entirely convincing. It is an awkward and unsettling
picture designed to induce a personal meditation on the wages of sin.

1. See Robert Hughes discussion of 'Les Demoiselles d' Avignon' in *The Shock of the New*, BBC, London, 1980. p 24
2. John Berger *Ways of Seeing*, Pelican, London, 1975. p 50
3. Although as Roger Grainger suggests in *The Language of the Rite*, 1974 (quoted in the introductory essay), this device can work
    to make 'past and future, near and far, fact and fantasy, present.'

PSALM 5

Oil on canvas, 61 x 76.5 cm., 1976

'FOR THOU, LORD, WILT BLESS THE RIGHTEOUS: WITH FAVOUR WILT THOU COMPASS HIS AS WITH A SHIELD.' Verse 12

As a Catholic, Zofrea understands that this simple meal can be read as an act of communion with God. God is embodied in the loaf of bread and the figs and his presence is acknowledged in the woman's expression of inner peace and serenity. The sense of sharing that is integral to the act of communion is also a major component of the meal and these two figures are shown at the moment of giving thanks for their repast.

In fact, the prayer the woman offers is another direct transcription from *Verse 3*, '… in the morning I will direct *my prayer* unto thee, and will look up.' It is a simple image which the artist has infused with a deeply felt spirituality. Once again the source for this imagery is a distant childhood memory of a shared meal in Borgia, Calabria when the artist was a young boy.

The contained and familiar space depicted in the painting is a recreation of that protective, nurturing environment and, as in many of Zofrea's paintings, the material density with which he invests these visual memories conjures up a very convincing image.

Although not a contrived likeness, the caring, devoted mother figure at the centre of the composition does represent the artist's mother and in turn *all* mothers. She is the fulcrum around which the family revolves and sitting in her kitchen she is in her domain. It is this image of security, nurture and protection that the artist draws from the Psalm. At the same time Zofrea acknowledges that the dark clad figure might also be a priest so the more formal connection with Holy communion is also reinforced; even though it is the woman who seems destined to break the bread. As the two focal points of the composition are the hands and the uncut loaf of bread the anticipation is palpable in the technical construction of the image.

We are constantly drawn back to the central figure because of the clever innovation of emphasising the gradual blurriness of peripheral vision. The mother figure is solid and in sharp focus in the centre of our field of vision, her solid, fleshy hands hovering three centimetres above her plate, but as we move out from the centre each element becomes less and less distinct until the 'priest's' chair dissolves into a thin veil of stained colour. This creates a vortex that keeps drawing us back into the centre.

In the tradition of Baroque religious imagery, Zofrea insists that we are involved in the events he describes by offering insights into the psychology of devotion, and by structuring the paintings to concur with our physical reality. Hence the simulation of our modes of seeing and the crowded picture plane that presses us closer to the action. This is one of the simplest and most tender of the early Psalms and its quiet reverence may well have accorded with the artist's state of mind after his illness.

STUDY FOR PSALM 6
Watercolour on paper, 30 x 45.7 cm., 1976

'RETURN, O LORD, DELIVER MY SOUL: OH SAVE ME FOR THY MERCIES' SAKE.'
Verse 4

There are affinities between this work and *Psalm 1*. Both show a man tending his garden as a metaphor for communion with God. The garden has a traditional symbolic meaning as an image of the primal, sin-free condition of humanity and within Zofrea's own symbology it is further extended to include his father's preoccupation with productivity and on occasions to represent the distance that existed between them. This *Psalm* combines several of these interpretations which are given an unusually close focus by the artist. In the earlier painting we are placed in the position of the ungodly, separated from the activity of the gardener tending his blooms by a wire mesh fence. The intensely close focus of this painting, which he began painting a year later when he was in a buoyant mood after recovering his health, indicates a greater optimism and trust in the benefits of prayer. The old man has his eyes closed in quiet meditation as he genuflects among the lilies in his garden.

Not surprisingly, Zofrea has chosen the flowers which the Bible mentions as a symbol of trusting devotion in God, 'Consider the lilies of the field ... even Solomon in all his glory was not arrayed like one of these' (*St Matthew 6:28*), so the old man is presented as the embodiment of this trusting devotion.

The intimacy of this view is guaranteed by the compositional device of filling the picture frame to overflowing with the man and the flowers and placing the viewer at eye level with the man and his blooms. It encourages us to share his silent reverie and like him we are asked to 'Consider the lilies ...' and count ourselves amongst the righteous. In other words we are also on our knees in the garden sharing this moment of quiet contemplation.

A comparison between the watercolour study and the final painting of the *Psalm* is very instructive in this instance. The study is a landscape format in which the blooms that spread off to the right of the composition command more of our attention than the figure. When developing the final version this format is changed to be more like a square because it draws us into closer contact with the gardener and places the lilies more resolutely between us. There is more space above the figure in the study which indicates a lower vantage point for the viewer and, though still close, a greater distance from him. By cropping the image so tightly in the oil painting, Zofrea has brought us within centimetres of his face and his heavy, work hardened hands. One of the smallest paintings in the series, it is nevertheless a work of great intensity that involves us completely in its simple narrative.

S. ZOFREA

PSALM 7

Oil on canvas, 101.6 x 132.2 cm., 1976

'O LORD MY GOD, IN THEE DO I PUT MY TRUST: SAVE ME FROM ALL THAT
PERSECUTE ME, AND DELIVER ME:' Verse 1

The Baroque artist's use of an infinite prolongation of space to suggest a metaphysical vantage point functioned as a means of focusing the viewer's mind away from
material and onto metaphysical problems. The implications of the everyday could
be cast aside enabling them to deal with the grand themes of life, death and the
spirit. Simple objects such as an open window or a single lit candle have an iconographic significance that supplant the commonplace and charge the picture
with a spiritual energy drawing the viewer into a world of contemplation and
meditation.

In *Psalm 7* Zofrea confronts his illness and the reaffirmation of his Catholicism so by adopting a similar form of pervasive perspective to that used by the
Baroque artists he suggests that his audience join him in his quest. He sets the
viewer free to hover in space and move like a spectre through various rooms and
then out to a distant horizon.

Based on the house and garden of his friend Geoffrey Lehmann, the action
takes place simultaneously but separately in two rooms of the house. An open window into the room, where three figures wait, indicates the presence of Christ who
has passed through unseen to visit the sick man (Zofrea) in his bed. The curtain
still flaps to indicate his passing, even though the other occupants are unaware that
the spiritual visitation is occurring.

Zofrea's ability to bring together the aspects of his personal life with his compulsion to illustrate the Psalms links him to Breughel and Stanley Spencer, who
both described the events of the Bible as extensions of their family and village life.
For Zofrea the village is Borgia and the particular scriptures that have meaning for
him are the Psalms while for Spencer his milieu was Cookham, in Berkshire, and
the New Testament stories of Christ and the resurrection take centre stage. More
importantly though, they are both storytellers who use the Biblical stories as a way
of venting personal anxieties and seeking salvation. Rather than set up a narrative
around a well known theme such as the Last Supper or Christ on the Cross, as a
Renaissance painter might have done, Spencer and Zofrea extemporise on a set
text and amplify its meaning through a personal exploration. Nevertheless, the full
meaning of the picture is almost impossible to draw out from the painting without
some knowledge of the text illustrated.

In *Psalm 7* dedicating one's life to God, so beautifully evoked in the text, is
given added poignancy by the artist's translation of the message to an event in his
own life. The burgeoning world of flowers and fruitfulness outside the window
presages his reward of a happy and fulfilled life which, he believes, will follow this
act of dedication. The message to us all is simple and brings the Psalms into the
orbit of our own lives.

PSALM 8

NOAH'S ARK
Oil on canvas, 198 x 274 cm., 1976

'THOU MADEST HIM TO HAVE DOMINION OVER THE WORKS OF THY HANDS ...'
(Verse 6), '... THE BEASTS OF THE FIELD;' (Verse 7), 'THE FOWL OF THE AIR,
AND THE FISH OF THE SEA ...' (Verse 8)

Zofrea chooses to illustrate humanity's dominion over the creatures of the earth
with the story of Noah and his ark. Once again the theme he elicits from the Psalm
is the need to turn to God and to seek his protection and nurture despite the deri-
sion or indifference of others. After his illness and the loss of two important figures
in his life (his mother and Henry Justelius) it is not surprising that he should see
this as the central message of so many of the early Psalms.

Though he later succumbed to drunkenness and turned away from God,
Noah's stewardship of the animals and birds makes this a perceptive and informa-
tive selection of subject matter. Zofrea sets Noah's search for beasts and fowl for
the ark at the beach at Clontarf, Sydney where he is watched idly by a seated
bather, two elderly people in deckchairs and a recumbent couple, who seem totally bemused by the whole event. Despite the world shattering implications prefig-
ured by Noah's quest there is an atmosphere of matter-of-fact indifference that is
emphasised by the playing children and the figure looking fixedly out to sea. As in
the previous Psalm the artist is keen to highlight the unsuspected occurrence of
momentous spiritual events in the most prosaic settings.

The veracity of these events is given more weight by the meticulous detail
that not only situates the bathers in their time and place, but by association gives
material density to the Biblical stories. The cast shadows and billowing support of
the deckchairs and the pelican stretching forward to take the small fish in Noah's
hand are palpably real. Consequently the rather bizarre conjunction of the tunic
clad figure mustering his precious cargo does not seem out of place on Clontarf
beach. Indeed the disinterest, even disdain, Noah met from the Cainites is emu-
lated here by the Sydney-siders of this century.

It is this blending of purely documentary visual details with the imaginative
constructions of his 'mind's eye' that gives Zofrea's paintings of the Psalms their
intensity and convincing presence. The detail gives weight to the imagined forms
and the emotional conviction of his Biblical transpositions dramatises what might
be read as rather banal renderings of natural form. In combination they make the
extraordinary a part of the everyday, demystifying the Bible and presenting it as a
practical guide for living one's life. This is certainly how the artist felt about the
Psalms when he first read them and it is why the enormous project of completing
the entire 150 still sustains him.

PSALM 9
Oil on canvas, 71.2 x 96.5 cm., 1976

'I WILL BE GLAD AND REJOICE IN THEE: I WILL SING PRAISE TO THEY NAME, O THOU MOST HIGH.' Verse 2

Zofrea was brought up in a household where rearing your own food and keeping the family sustained on freshly picked produce was an essential ingredient of everyday life. Domesticated birds pecked around the back door of the house and his father was often busy in the extensive vegetable garden. Not surprisingly then, this image of harmony with nature and the cyclical pattern of growth and harvesting has deep associations with family life for the artist and when addressing the central theme of the search for security expressed in this Psalm, he returned to the image of a young man in a garden. Seated under the dappled shade of a tree the young man is perfectly at peace with his environment. Gardens are often used as a metaphor for paradise on earth and as a symbol of cosmic order, so this image can be interpreted as another version of the peaceable kingdom predicted in *Isaiah 11*, 'The wolf also shall dwell with the lamb ...' In this ideal world the young man, about to serenade the birds with his flute, will use music to 'sing praise' to God for the harmony and order he finds in the universe.

In the first year after his recovery from the illness that instigated his project of painting all of the Psalms, the promise of peace, order and security was made manifest in his renewed health. In one very real sense then, this painting could be seen as a *Per Gracia Ricevuta* image, like those found throughout churches in Italy. The faithful pray to their patron Saint and on receipt of their prayers they make a small painting or object which describes that beneficence. The images are inscribed PGR (for grace received).

Zofrea clearly associates with the young man in his painting and gives thanks for the security his parents provided and the sense of being at one with the forces of cosmic order. He also invokes Saint Francis and his sermon to the birds and draws the familiar comparison between earthly and heavenly paradise. In Christian iconography birds are often depicted as the mediators between heaven and earth and communion with the fowl of the air is therefore one way of establishing direct contact with God.

The bulk of the figure and the shallow pictorial space recalls the early Renaissance painters. Birds and foliage are laid out around the central figure, as if painted onto a backdrop, so that their clearly delineated shapes form a pattern out of which the simply rendered volumes of the young man seem to swell up out of the painting. The contrast of small, coloured details surrounding the mass of the figure gives great weight and purpose to his every gesture.

Zofrea's interest in Giotto and the fresco painters of the *quattrocento* is an extremely important influence in these early works, and helps to explain his affinity with the English painter of religious themes, Stanley Spencer, who was also a significant influence in these early works.

PSALM 10

Oil on canvas, 61 x 45.7 cm., 1976

'LORD THOU HAST HEARD THE DESIRE OF THE HUMBLE: THOU WILT PREPARE THEIR HEART, THOU WILT CAUSE THINE EAR TO HEAR.' Verse 17

The quiet meditation of this woman as she prepares to eat her evening meal is transformed by the artist into a moment of great spiritual import. Bread has traditionally symbolised both spiritual nourishment and Christ, 'the living bread, which came from heaven', and that interpretation is at the heart of this small painting.

Just before she died, Zofrea remembers walking into the kitchen one afternoon and seeing his mother sitting alone at the table eating a simple meal of pears and bread. 'I found that so moving', he explains, 'so moving that it upsets me even now'. Whether as a premonition of his mother's death or as a confirmation of her commanding presence in the family, this event became deeply etched in his visual memory. When illustrating Psalm 10 with its message of protection for humble people from the evil that is inflicted upon them, he epitomised their strength and their suffering in the image of his mother praying over her evening meal.

There is an interesting comparison to be drawn between this image and *Psalm 5*, in which his mother is once again seated at a table near a window eating her meal. In that case the dark figure to the left of the picture, who is about to share the communion of the meal, reinforces the more formal connection with Holy Communion. In this *Psalm* the woman is alone with her thoughts in a private contemplation of the trials of her life. While the first picture was set in the morning, this painting depicts early evening as an indication of the triumph of life over all obstacles. It is also more solid in form, every detail rendered with care to establish the concrete reality and physical weight of the moment. The light which enters from the window assists in this task and gives further significance to this reading because the light is also symbolic of the presence of Christ in her life.

Zofrea links all of these ideas together within the paradox of a highly refined naivety which enables him to combine the rich colouring and clarity of the image with a sense of the ineffable. This mysterious element is also a product of the convergence of memory and of the observation that generated it. Some elements are drawn from life, others are constructed from the rich source of his visual memory and the combination creates an intensity of vision that has great power because of its immediacy and lack of sentiment.

A small painting by Zofrea's standards, this Psalm has the presence of an icon or a devotional picture. Our attraction toward the figure, which he contrives through the insistent linear perspective of the table, and the massive weight of her hands hovering above the end of the table, bring us into a familial relationship with her. From the viewpoint we are asked to adopt it is clear that we are sitting at the other end of the table, even though she is distanced from us by her meditation on past suffering. We can only empathise with and admire her resilience.

BOEKER PSLAM NO. 10

PSALM 11
Oil on canvas, 71 x 91.5 cm., 1976

'IN THE LORD PUT I MY TRUST: HOW SAY YE TO MY SOUL, FLEE AS A BIRD TO YOUR MOUNTAIN?' Verse 1

Painted in his studio bedroom at the family home in Seaforth, this is the only painting in the series that does not include human figures. Of course the presence of human intelligence and handiwork is everywhere; in the delicately stitched patterning on the curtains, the structure of the window frame, the organisation of the garden and even the fence that runs along the horizon. Indeed the viewer is placed within the structure of a dwelling to contemplate the garden which is separated from us by the closed window.

In this case the narrative is carried by the inconspicuous ladybird resting on the window frame. Instead of the bird referred to in the Psalm, the artist recalling that the ladybird must 'fly away, fly away home' in the nursery rhyme, makes the appropriate change to suggest the flight to God. It will not be easy because the ladybird is so frail and small, the way is barred by the closed window and there are dangers and distractions ahead in the deliciously scented magnolia and many unseen predators. Nevertheless, the artist's conviction to put his trust in God, despite the difficulties, is given an indelible presence in this painting.

It is worth remembering that the open window, found in *Psalm 7*, indicated the presence of Christ, so the closed window in this picture may suggest that the journey has not yet begun and the ladybird is unable to commit herself fully until she has accepted Christ.

In many of the paintings the objective world is transformed by the artist to serve the narrative function of the Psalm and to embody the metaphysical dimension of the text, however in this painting the artist is not interested in imposing his own creative intelligence. The purely documentary reportage of the scene, though quite lyrical, is an attempt to be as veracious as possible. The delicacy of his treatment of this scene does evoke an atmosphere of calm, however, and the soft, early morning light, a faint breeze and the indication of the heavily scented flower does suggest a sensoria that is common to much of the artist's work. We are encouraged to provide those additional stimuli from our memory to complete the scene he describes.

Nature and the ebb and flow of the seasons are extremely important in Zofrea's *oeuvre* because the natural world is itself linked to the larger Christian tradition through the lunar calendar. This determines Saint's days and religious festivals and also serves as a guide to planting and growing seasons. Any Italian farmer or gardener, like the artist's father, knows when to plant his crops from the festivities announced each Sunday at Mass. This closely woven pattern of life and faith is intrinsic to Zofrea's art.

PSALM 12

SONG OF SONGS (SONG OF SOLOMON)
Oil on canvas, 152.5 x 183 cm., 1976

'THE WORDS OF THE LORD ARE PURE WORDS: AS SILVER ... PURIFIED SEVEN TIMES' Verse 6

In this Psalm Zofrea brings together the erotic imagery of *The Song of Solomon* with the celebration of God's word. It is the first of the images of a bountiful and harmonious Heaven where those rewarded for their faith find peace and pleasure. There is little of the punitive aspects of the Judaeo-Christian tradition in Zofrea's images of heaven. Although this Psalm contains many descriptions of the terrible things that will befall the wicked or weak, Zofrea identifies the positive power of God's word and grafts it onto the pleasures of the flesh celebrated in *The Song of Solomon*. Consequently the images of embracing couples rolling amongst the flowers and birds are linked to the central figure's outstretched salutation to the magpie, used here as an image of God.

The glass beads that form an arch above the bird's head are contrived as an image of the stars in heaven and the glimpses of a fertile landscape rolling on to the horizon are a setting appropriate to both seduction and salutation. All the images of heaven in Zofrea's work are a joyous celebration of life.

The large, almost pneumatic, figures that swell to fill the picture are closely related to the solid figures in Giotto's frescoes and the rustic villagers of Cookham in Stanley Spencer's great religious paintings. They are linked by an entwining arabesque that runs through the flowers and the patterned dresses which wrap them in a tight jig-saw of colour and line. Like Spencer, whose influence in these early pictures the artist willingly acknowledges, the awkwardness of their generalised shape contrasts with the precise detail and accurate depiction of the flowers, birds and landscape. This juxtaposition, though disturbing and on occasions uncomfortably awkward, is so sincerely rendered that it works to affirm intensely felt meaning. In much the same way naive artists like Henri Rousseau or the Italian villagers making their *Per Gracia Ricevuta* images, give added significance to their images.

The figures have a weight that is not only physically but also emotionally convincing. His interest in objects (people, flowers, birds, leaves, patterns) for their own sake means that his pictures often have the look of a collection of elements laid down like a jig-saw. Each is interesting in its own right, not because of its relationship to any other object or because of its incidental importance to an overall atmosphere or set of colour relationships. They are described with precise outlines and sharp colours to establish them as *things*. One consequence of this *modus operandi* is that in this version of heaven there is no envelope[1] of light or colour to surround and hold figures, flowers and birds, instead they are merely set like gems, separate from each other, yet contributing to a rich pattern of life.

---

1.   See Anna Waldmann's essay in *Salvatore Zofrea*, Stephanie Claire and Anna Waldmann, Hale & Iremonger, Sydney, 1983, for her description of this effect in Zofrea's work.

PSALM 13
OPENING OF THE FIFTH SEAL
Oil on canvas, 76 x 51 cm., 91 x 61 cm., 76 x 51 cm., (triptych), 1976

'HOW LONG SHALL I TAKE COUNSEL IN MY SOUL … HOW LONG SHALL MINE ENEMY BE EXALTED OVER ME?' *Verse 2*

The opening of the fifth seal in *The Revelations of St John the Divine* describes how the souls of the martyrs rise up and ask God why he does not '… judge and avenge our blood on them that dwell on the earth.' It echoes the message in *Verse 2* of this Psalm, however the imagery which Zofrea illustrates in his painting is taken from *Revelation 6:11*

> And white robes were given unto every one of them: and it was said unto every one of them, that they should rest …

So although God agrees to take retribution, the punitive aspect of the narrative is put to one side to highlight the importance of following God's commands.

Zofrea fills the space with figures preparing to don the white robes brought down by angels, who appear from the top-most section of the picture. In the shallowest of pictorial spaces, reminiscent of Giotto's frescoes, the figures stand cheek by jowl within the confining space of the painting. This is made to seem even more compressed by their size. Unlike any other martyrs represented in art these are definitely the 'lumpy proletariat', people off the street in Borgia, Calabria or Seaforth, Australia, their forms inflated and disproportionately emphasised. In particular their hands are huge and heavy to give weight to their entreaties.

The figures are unified by a low key colouration of whites, browns and ochres, highlighted with touches of red, blue and yellow in the patterned dresses and related to each other by a rhythm of echo lines that emanate from the central panel in which St John is surrounded by kneeling figures pulling off their street clothes and climbing into the white robes. This harmonious play of shape, line and colour is orchestrated in the manner of a slow and insistent dirge.

It is instructive to compare this painting with Giotto's great fresco *The Death of St Francis* in the Bardi Chapel, Santa Croce, in Florence. Giotto places a Franciscan friar with his hands raised in grief at the centre of the composition and surrounds the death bed with groups of solidly real figures standing in a plausible but shallow space. Kneeling figures in the foreground and angels in the sky complete a circular movement which involves us in the passage from the temporal to the spiritual world. These same devices are the key to Zofrea's composition. Although he has added a narrative distortion of the forms and a complementary rhythm of pattern and colour in the dresses of the women, the same gravity of meaning and form is evident as restrained emotions are revealed through the slow and measured gestures of the supplicants.

The monumentality he achieves through a compelling simplicity and directness makes this one of the most powerful and moving of the early Psalms.

PSALM 14

QUE DICE DONNA DICE DONNA
Oil on canvas, 184 x 198 cm., 1978

'THEY ARE CORRUPT, THEY HAVE DONE ABOMINABLE WORKS, THERE IS NONE
THAT DOETH GOOD.' Verse 1

The bordello is a recurring image of the fall in Zofrea's work. Men succumbing to
their licentious natures and the detached women ministering to their pleasure not
only offer tremendous scope for the painter to show a range of attitudes and poses,
they give him the ideal arena in which to develop his narrative on the wages of sin.
In *Psalm 4* the client is almost out of view, so that the focus falls on the three prostitutes, but in this picture he selects as his central theme the parade when the girls of
the house are offered to the customers for their selection. Consequently the artist
involves the viewer directly in his narrative by citing them as accomplices.

Even the viewpoint they are forced to take is similar to the other clients. The
viewer is observing the action from a seated position on another red velvet seat on
the other side of the room. Although viewing is in most cases unthreatening it is
clear from the organisation of this painting that the artist will not allow his audience the pleasure of detachment. Staring fixedly at the floor in front of their feet,
the young girl in her underwear draws them further into the ambiance of the room
by her refusal to make eye-contact. As detached as her sisters in the previous painting, she carries out her delicate arm movements with awkward resignation and her
embarrassment, combined with the garish, overly plush surroundings and the
prurient gaze of the three customers, injects an uncomfortable silence into the
room. The awkward poses and forced smiles of the three clients adds to this sense
of indignity.

Pervading the whole scene is an unreal, fabricated sense of fertility embodied in the luxuriant paintings of flowers and birds and the rugs, wallpaper and
lamps that mimic the forms and patterns of nature but do not retain its productivity or fecundity. The only 'real' plant in the room is a dark, green palm behind the
girl which supports her and seems to join in her stilted dance. If nature is aligned
with the young girl, the old men in their 'spivy' suits and loud ties are obviously
associated in the artist's programme with the essentially retrograde depictions of
virility and growth. Only the impressively erect sprouting marble statue, with its
minute Venus perched on top, stands tall as a painful memory of their lost youth.

This painting seems extraordinarily colourful amongst the earlier thirteen
Psalms because it initiates a stronger role for pure colour as an expressive tool. The
subdued colours of the earlier works, although enlivened by touches of brighter
colour, suggest a unified and calm environment where human beings are at peace
with nature. This work and many that follow, show the schism that has occurred to
separate humanity from its roots in Nature; a rupture the artist would convince us
is only healed in heaven.

PSALM 15

TE DEUM
Oil on canvas (triptych), 229 x 604 cm., 1978

'LORD, WHO SHALL ABIDE IN THY TABERNACLE?' (Verse 1) HE THAT WORKETH
UPRIGHTLY AND WORKETH RIGHTEOUSNESS AND SPEAKETH THE TRUTH IN HIS
HEART.' (Verse 2)

This massive painting is a joyous celebration of life. Like the *Te Deum*, which gives
it its name, it is a hymn of praise to God and an image of heaven that echoes *Psalm
3* and *Psalm 12* and prefigures the image of heaven in *Psalm 24*. It is also a marriage
of humanity with nature that shows a bond between people and places intrinsic to
Zofrea's work.

Some figures are entwined in the bounty of magnolia, jasmine, arum lilies
and dahlias, others fall into each others' arms in a curving arch that echoes the
shape of the hills and all are embedded in the landscape and grow out of it, because
they are seen as an extension of Nature. In heaven everyone is young and at peace
with each other and as we have seen in the earlier painting, *Psalm 12 — Song of
Songs (Song of Solomon)*, the idea of heaven is also linked in Zofrea's imagery with
the erotic. The gyrating, swirling sense of adoration and celebration is therefore
expressed as another aspect of social intercourse. People couple, talk with each
other, read sacred texts, play musical instruments and nurture their children as an
amplification of their praise for God. These various aspects are drawn together by a
complex mix of stylistic influences and pictorial experimentation.

Like the French 'primitive' painter Henri Rousseau, Zofrea combines the
sincere *gaucherie* of the naive painter with a razor sharp clarity of forms and a highly
pitched colouration. At the same time the convergence of memory and observation, as tools to generate imagery, reinforce this sense of visionary explication. It is
as if the secrets of heaven were being revealed to us with all the sincerity and
wonder of a young children reciting their Sunday School lessons. The images from
memory, such as the portraits of family and friends, are cobbled together with the
objective studies of flowers and landscape with a similar naive charm. These are
then welded together by the artist's ability to achieve a rhythmic unity in his paintings and by his concern for creating surface patterning which brings the forms
together in a convincing way. This blend of naive vision and sophistication enables
him to credit the traditions of the Renaissance while retaining his own idiosyncratic vision.

A flavour of the early Renaissance is injected by the deployment of the
figures throughout the composition and the hieratic placement of Christ at the
centre, while his insistence on documenting the smallest details of Nature is reminiscent of Botticelli and the Lorenzetti brothers. The integration of the figures
into a tightly controlled formal jig-saw of landscape and flowers also harks back to
the early Renaissance which, by implication, suggests a concurrence with Dante's
Paradiso. Zofrea's images are never completely contemporary, they are either
situated in his childhood in Calabria or placed within his own fabrication of the
Renaissance. This introduces a veil of memory that induces a more reflective
reading and encourages quiet meditation on the themes he presents.

PSALM 16

Oil on canvas, 150 x 180 cm., 1988

'FOR THOU WILT NOT LEAVE MY SOUL IN HELL …' (Verse 10) 'THOU WILT SHEW ME THE PATH OF LIFE … AT THY RIGHT HAND THERE ARE PLEASURES FOR EVERMORE.' (Verse 11)

Although it looks like another painting of a bordello the artist describes the setting of this moral tale as the family home. Within this domestic interior the three ages of humanity are represented by the young boy, the couple exploring their sexuality and the older woman. They form a continuum within the 'dance of life/death' that is the central theme of the painting. The old woman who has seen it all before, is at the end of her life while the innocent young boy is fascinated by this display of sexual coupling. Clearly for Zofrea it is an event that implies both the continuation of life and its end. Life may be a dance of joyous celebration but it leads inexorably to the dance of death, that familiar mediaeval picture-subject of Death leading all ranks to the grave. This image of mortality, pressing in on the most fundamental of human experiences, is extremely unsettling and Zofrea has maintained this sense of anxiety in the painting by creating a dark environment in which all the characters are spotlit by the large standard lamp or the unseen light source just off-stage.

Theatrical lighting is a frequent tool in his paintings and in this Psalm he also adopts other devices of the stage and screen. He mimics a cinematic pan that carries us around the action, lingering on the faces, the bodies and the reactions of each character. He then makes use of the mid-shot and close-up to draw us closer into their world. In fact some of these images are even borrowed from film stills.

The Psalm teaches that those that follow God's teaching will find joy, however, the imagery implies a much less positive message. Although the young couple will undoubtedly find pleasure the older woman's expression implies that she knows the dangers and pit-falls they will encounter and within this moral context the two faces of world weariness and innocence are established as the polar extremes of the path suggested by the groping entanglement of the young lovers. They are neither to be envied nor pitied for their choice represents the thin line between innocence and experience where sexuality is a force that is felt if not fully understood.

It may be that Zofrea is reflecting on this key moment in his own or any human's life and using it to advise his audience that for him the only answer is to follow the teachings of the Psalms. 'Therefore my heart is glad … my flesh also shall rest in hope.' He injects a note of poignancy by placing himself into the painting as the image of innocence. The young boy with the open face is painted from a photograph of Zofrea acting as a page boy at his sister's wedding in Borgia. This is the first of a series of three paintings of dark interiors that compress the moral messages of the Psalms into the domestic environment of the artist's recreation of his childhood home in Calabria, and what appears to be an Italian bar. After the joyous imagery of *Psalm 15* they are darkly foreboding.

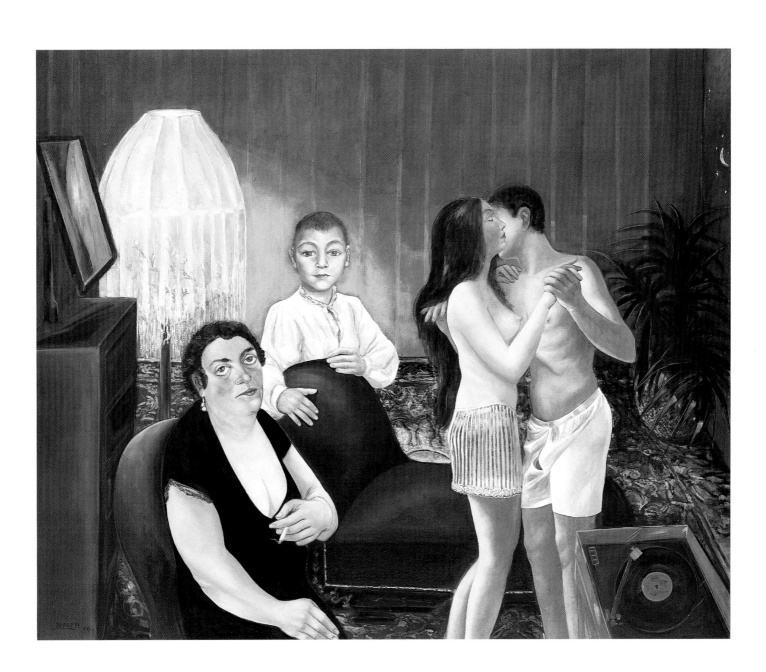

PSALM 17
Oil on canvas, 195 x 300 cm., 1988

'... HIDE ME UNDER THE SHADOW OF THY WINGS ...' (Verse 8) 'FROM THE WICKED THAT OPPRESS ME ...' (Verse 9)

As a small child in Calabria Zofrea was not weaned from his mother's breast until he was three and a half. Known to be a good 'sucker', he was asked to suckle the breasts of a neighbour having difficulties feeding her baby because her milk would not flow. He struck a bargain that he would suckle for a week in return for a religious painting hanging over her bed. When the task had been completed, the woman claimed the painting was lost and refused to keep her part of the bargain. This deceit struck hard at the young Zofrea's sense of morality and remained a key memory for the next thirty years. When searching out imagery to illustrate this Psalm it once again re-surfaced.

It is a significant memory because it brings together his passion for art and his sense of moral outrage at being exploited. Not surprisingly he found it a highly appropriate core around which to construct a complex narrative on the theme of seduction and deceit. The artist appears in the centre of the painting suckling the breasts of a recumbent woman, below him another boy mimics his position while engaged in a phallic game with a fox-headed boy. The comparisons he draws between the innocence of infantile sexual contact and the eroticism of the older boys and the young man fondling the breasts of his girlfriend rekindles his belief in the inexorable fall of humanity. It is a recurring theme in Zofrea's *Psalms*, where the 'fall' becomes a symbol for humanity's weakness and where trust in God is offered as the only solution. As if to prove this point the painting on the wall shows Christ after his crucifixion still offering comfort to those that deceived him. As in the previous *Psalm* the artist is exploring the borders between innocence and experience where sexuality is a force that acts as a driver even though we neither understand it nor query its power. Not surprisingly they are both night pictures.

This concern is also extended to other fundamental human responses, such as nourishment. At the back of the room three men seek their nourishment by picking over the bones of a chicken, oblivious to the boy at the breast, while two women hold their children in a protective embrace. Nurturing and nourishment are further contrasted in the way the sexual embrace of the young couple is juxtaposed with the mother holding her children.

The relationship between these figures is given more weight because of the stifling overcrowding. The interior becomes a containing device for the totality of human experience and the pressure on the picture plane draws us into these relationships as co-conspirators. Zofrea effectively opens himself up to his own fears and anxieties and through his art he manages to perpetuate his childhood visions and to give them an epic quality rather like a village Passion Play.

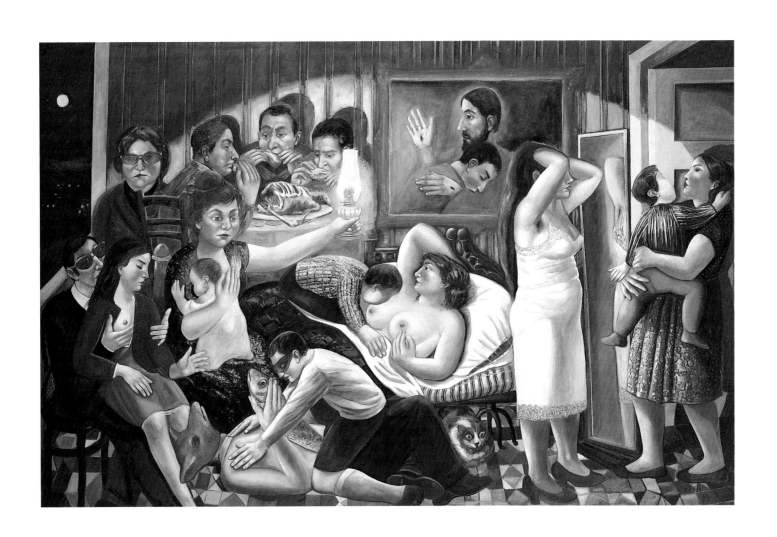

PSALM 18

LA NOTTE DI ROSIGNANO
Oil on canvas, 180 x 240 cm., 1987

'FOR THOU WILT LIGHT MY CANDLE: THE LORD MY GOD WILL ENLIGHTEN MY
DARKNESS' Verse 28

In the last of three nocturnal interiors that deal with the theme of sexuality, deceit
and temptation, the action is located in a public cafe. The most immediate consequence of this change from the domestic environment of the first two paintings is
the expanded sense of space that isolates individuals and groups, however the
darkened spaces and internal light sources creates a similarly disquieting atmosphere. 'At night more things happen' explains the artist, and while much is hid-
den by the darkness, night light offers the chance to spotlight these activities. The
five separate incidents described in the painting chronicle different states of
human interaction. The social discourse undertaken by the threesome on the right
is contrasted with the solitary young man in the foreground, and the lovers slow
waltz is played-off against the single girl's energetic solo. In the final visual inci-
dent, the cat licks up the milk, drinking its full from the saucer (of life?), surrounded by an empty bottle, a spilt glass and smoked cigarettes.

Some of paintings from this series are set in the distant past of the artist's
childhood in Calabria while others occupy a neutral past where there are no televisions, motor cars or electrical goods. This painting could be read as a simple cafe
but its 'other worldliness' is suggested by a similar distanced history evoked by the
strange luminescence which pervades the set (an eerie ambience that the artist
might have borrowed from Fassbinder's disquieting film *Querelle*). When combined with the upturned parrot it is clear that all is not well. 'The Lord will enlight-
en my darkness', presumably from the 'wickedness' described in the rest of the
picture?

Once again the image of a single lighted candle is symbolic of the presence of
Christ and the open book is included to represent the word of God. The young
man, staring out at us with an expression of self assurance seems to be strength-
ened by these supports and, we assume, is therefore safe from the 'dangers' lurk-
ing in the shadows. The room becomes not only a site of temptation but also one of
redemption, even though it is the activities described here as 'wicked', or at least a
diversion from the true path recommended by the *Psalms*, that take centre stage.

Another theatrical device employed in all three *Psalms* is the inclusion of a
figure who seeks out eye contact with us, either as a attempt to elicit our support or
as a clear message that the reality of the painting is merely an extension of ours. It
shakes us from our role as distanced viewer in much the same way that Brecht's
'Alienation Effect' was designed to shock his audience out of their secure indifference. This theatrical device is an extension of the Baroque concept of involvement which suggests a universality that might otherwise be missed because of the
'other worldliness' of the situations and places described.

PSALM 19

LA GRANDE PROMESSA
Oil on canvas, 180 x 270 cm., 1987

'... CLEANSE THOU ME FROM MY SECRET FAULTS.' (Verse 12). 'LET THE WORDS OF MY MOUTH, AND THE MEDITATION OF MY HEART, BE ACCEPTABLE IN THY SIGHT, O LORD, MY STRENGTH AND MY REDEEMER'. (Verse 14)

Zofrea did not paint the *Psalms* in numerical order. *Psalm 23* was painted in the same year as *Psalm 14* and *Psalms 22–28* were painted four years later in 1982, two years before *Psalms 15–17*. He did not return to the project for another three years when he undertook *Psalms 18, 20, 21* and this painting, the first of a series based on photographs of a busker he had seen in Florence. Just after he saw the busker and took numerous photographs of his performance, the artist heard that his father was dying and cut short his tour of Italy to return to Australia.

The pain of watching his father die was so intense that Zofrea sought relief in painting the Psalms and turned to those that dealt with the theme of God's promise of redemption. In the face of his father's death he subtitled this Psalm, *La Grande Promessa (The Great Promise)*. Within the context of the previous paintings these starkly presented images in intensely bright colours mark an abrupt change in the artist's approach to illustrating the Psalms. The nocturnal images with their strong internal lighting were very cinematic, these pictures in contrast adopt devices from the theatre. The acknowledgment of the artifice of the stage with its flimsy back cloth, bright, unmodulated colour and straightforward frontal presentation in a shallow space opened up new avenues in exploring his ideas on the superficiality of life without belief and the transitory nature of our existence.

The young busker putting his animals through their painful trials proved to be a potent image which enabled the artist to accommodate his sense of disorientation and pain. 'It was painful and I realised how I could use these images in my depiction of the Psalms to show how we exploit life and exploit each other.'[1] The cat on its swing, the goat with its ridiculous pompom and the caged bird, represent humanity being put through the trial of existence by a group of buskers and circus folk.

Zofrea is attracted to these people because they recall his childhood, when circus people and gypsies would arrive in Borgia on feast days. They also represent the duality of human existence because they mask their true feelings. The conjunction of the circus people with religious celebration has its roots in Borgia but it is used over and over again as a way of explaining the division that exists between the spiritual and the temporal. On earth people mask their feelings and suffer the trials of existence, but in heaven, according to Zofrea, there is no need to be duplicitous and all trials cease. The lights strung above this scene are a recurring symbol of heaven or the prospect of salvation in heaven, which the artist reminds us, is at hand. Below is the temporal world of trial and punishment, of disorientation and pain, but above it all is God's promise of redemption, his great promise.

1. See the interview with Zofrea in this volume.

Psalm 20
The Visitors
Oil on canvas, 180 x 270 cm., 1987

'They are brought down and fallen; but we are risen and stand upright': (Verse 8) 'Save, Lord; let the king hear us when we call': (Verse 9)

The warmer colours and the windows, opening out from the stage flat of the back-drop behind the figures on the right of this picture, generate a superficially lighter and more comfortable environment than the first painting in the 'busker' series. To enhance this feeling, music pervades the scene through the presence of the trumpet being playing on the left of the composition, and the goat has been goaded into action. It seems more festive and less threatening. This impression does not last too long however, for the screaming ape soon injects a raucous note and the exchanged glances between the observers casts a pall over the proceedings. What is happening? Why is it so awkward? The visitors of the title have arrived to see the show put on by the busker and from behind his odd assortment of stands and hoops they wait for the handcuffed and screeching ape to jump through a fiery hoop. His trainer is the young prostitute from *Psalm 14 — Que Dice Donna Dice Donna* who is trying to drag him through with a lead while she nonchalantly fondles a cat, who drinks from a saucer held by another spectator.

The detached gaze of each of the participants and their audience emphasises the agony of the ape, whose pain is of so little concern to anyone but itself. Zofrea was still recovering from the shock of his father's death and pondering on the transitory nature of human existence when he painted this picture and the ape came to stand for the crisis of his father's death and his hope for redemption. This is also the subject of the lines from the Psalm which he has chosen to illustrate. Once again the string of lights hung across the top of the picture evokes the presence of heaven as a sign of God's promise of redemption for those who suffer cruelty or pain. The presence of the visitors, in their role as an audience, reinforces his belief that it is impossible to affect other people's lives or to save them from suffering. It reflects the pain Zofrea felt for his father. Just as the spectators to this cruel performance can only watch and then walk on to be replaced by another audience and another and another, the artist could only sit and watch his father die.

His interest in the early Renaissance accounts for the appeal of the fully rounded volumes of the figures and it may have influenced his adoption of a greater clarity of the forms. Each is precisely outlined and brightly coloured in the manner of the Sienese artists of the *quattrocento* such as Pietro and Ambrogio Lorenzetti, whose mural *The Effects of Good and Bad Government* in the Palazzo Publico in Siena, has a solidity of form, a clarity and brilliance of colour and an emotional depth that is reflected in the formal qualities of this painting. More importantly, Zofrea has been able to fuse these formal qualities with the experiences of his own life to create a powerful meditation of the theme of this Psalm.

Psalm 21

Il Padrone
Oil on canvas, 150 x 165 cm., 1987

'For the king trusteth in the Lord, and through the mercy of the most High he shall not be moved': (Verse 1). 'Thine hand shall find out all thine enemies ...': (Verse 8): 'For they intended evil against thee ...': (Verse 10).

This is the most claustrophobic painting of the 'busker' series Zofrea produced after the death of his father. Unlike the preceding two *Psalms* in which the forms are deployed across an open stage, the crowding of the picture plane focuses attention on the act of aggression about to be carried out by the king. With his out-sized crown he is almost a direct translation of the central figure in *Psalm 2* but in this episode he is poised to light the flaming hoop through which the screaming ape must jump. It is a frozen moment, a close-up in cinematic terminology, before the action begins in earnest and the trials of life are played out.

The woman is preparing herself for the performance in the traditional manner of the stage and the strident theatricality is evident in the bright, flatly applied colour, the shallow spatial depth and the arrangement of the busker's props. The narrative is more cinematic than theatrical however, and the sense of a zoom into the small match flame at the centre of the canvas develops a more intimate relationship with the characters than could be achieved with the all encompassing sweep of the two earlier works. This intimacy is the antithesis of the distance normally associated with royal authority, and by employing it Zofrea is able to subvert the notion of temporal power. The king is empowered by God, as the Psalm indicates, and he seems to initiate the trials we undertake, but the ultimate authority rests elsewhere. In other words, Zofrea is suggesting that those with temporal power will always find it extremely difficult to fill the crown of responsibility and service offered by God. In the suffering of the ape the artist sees humanity trapped between the false demands and trials instituted by the temporal authority of kings and politicians and their own 'base' sexual desires. It is clearly painful and life threatening yet, as Zofrea reiterates in many of these interpretations of the Psalms, there is a spiritual authority that offers final redemption.

The austere formality of this painting calls to mind the work of Piero della Francesca, the Italian painter of the early Renaissance . Zofrea is attracted to Piero and the artists once collectively referred to as the 'Italian Primitives' because their less decorative and more linear paintings are models of a prestigious art of the past that is essentially spiritual in origin. In his attempt to confront the great spiritual truths raised by the death of his father, he turned to works such as Piero's master-piece *The Legend of the True Cross*, with its blend of mystery and intensity, as an example of how complex figure compositions could be orchestrated to carry significant meanings in a manner that was straight forward and easily readable. The 'busker' paintings are a homage to this tradition and an acknowledgment that it retains its vitality.

PSALM 22
Oil on canvas, 198 x 259 cm., 1982

'MY GOD, MY GOD, WHY HAST THOU FORSAKEN ME?' Verse 1

In 1982 Zofrea returned to the Psalms after working for 18 months on a huge mural for the Fairfax Group. The scale of the *Sydney Morning Herald* mural and the complexity of combining so many figures into a coherent narrative was excellent training for his *Psalms*. Equally as important, the commission had come at a most propitious time when he was ready to take full advantage of the opportunities it offered. Recognition had also come through his two successes in the Sulman Prize in 1977 and 1979. Nevertheless, when he chose his next subject he turned to the lamentation which begins *Psalm 22*.

'My God, My God, why hast thou forsaken me?' is one of the most familiar lines in all the Psalms, possibly because most Christians have at some time questioned their fate in the face of what seems to be unjust retribution. The artist admits that of the group of *Psalms* painted in 1982 this was 'the most tormenting and spiritually demanding'[1]. His conception of the defiled woman surrounded by indifferent humanity is echoed by Christ's crucifixion, described in the large painted backdrop to this episode and given added resonance by Christ's own repetition of these lines on the cross. The shocking juxtaposition of eroticism with spirituality and suffering with indifference is a challenging and disturbing subject and Zofrea draws his audience into this debate through the often repeated device of including figures that make direct eye contact. It is particularly unsettling in this painting because the viewer must confront not only the naive young man, whose own pleasure will take precedence over another's suffering, and the indifferent bureaucrat who is orchestrating that suffering, but also the victim. Christ looks straight at us with what the artist describes as 'an expression of horrific anger'[2].

The two incidents are intertwined in this way as if to confirm the continuity of suffering and the concomitant search for a justification of the harshness of life. Although it is not unusual for Christ to be depicted as a representative for all suffering humanity, the blatant eroticism of Zofrea's comparison in this work and the passivity of both victims does inject a distasteful sense of inevitability that seems to preclude any acceptable resolution. It is further complicated by the complicity of the viewer who is encouraged to enjoy the blatant display of the girl's body while reviling themselves for doing so. The girl's lower torso glows in the surrounding gloom with such radiance that it is impossible not to linger on her physical attractiveness in the same way that the young man surveys the object of his pleasure.

It is a most disturbing picture that offers no consolation on earth except death; represented in the centre of the painting by a skull being inspected by a small dog.

1. *Salvatore Zofrea*, p. 65.
2. *Ibid.*

PSALM 23

Oil on canvas, 127 x 152 cm., 1978, Collection of the Vatican Museum, Rome

'THE LORD IS MY SHEPHERD.' Verse 1

The best known of all the Psalms, its message of reassurance and consolation was a comfort to Zofrea at a time of crisis in his own life. His bout of serious illness and the death of his mother were the catalysts for beginning the *Psalms* and in his reading of the texts he discovered the full range of his own reactions to these events. A comparison between the two *Psalms* painted in 1978 indicates the polarities of his thinking, from the image of debauchery and the frailty of humanity in *Psalm 14 — Que Dice Donna Dice Donna* to the image of peaceful reassurance and redemption in this painting. The different messages contained within these two paintings is conveyed not only in the narrative but in the choice of setting and colouration. While the first painting is set in a dimly lit interior, full of artifice and luridly coloured in red and emerald green, *Psalm 23* is set in a fertile landscape under a bright sun. The pervasive soft blue/green light suggests a calm, ordered world in which humanity will be nurtured and protected.

These polar extremes indicate the range of Zofrea's reactions to the despair and anxiety he was feeling at the time, and probably goes some way in accounting for his choice of the Psalms as a theme.

The idea of sending a painting to the Pope was suggested by Father George Baggio, a Scalabrinian missionary working in Sydney who had seen *Psalm 13* hanging in the parish church at Dee Why, Sydney, and felt that a gift to the new Pope by an Australian/Italian artist would be an appropriate gesture. Zofrea began work immediately and chose as his theme the best loved of all the Psalms.

The resulting picture is very openly painted in comparison with the other works from this period and whether it was because of the nature of the commission or the subject matter itself, he was able to create an image that is full of light and air. The open brushwork with which he describes the river and the banks of foliage, in combination with the pitch of the colour and the surging movement toward a distant horizon, suggest a quite different feeling from the claustrophobic spaces described in the other images of the *Psalms*. It is as if the entire picture plane has been exposed in the broad pan of a camera. The sense of personal involvement, intrinsic to Zofrea's approach, is maintained by the vantage point he adopts.

It is clear from this view of the action that while the audience of family and friends watch from the front the viewer is standing at the head of a long queue of people waiting to be baptised. Instead of being able to stand outside the action as a disinterested observer, the viewer is drawn into the painting as a participant. This is assisted by Zofrea's overall intention to present religion as an extension of his own family life. Hence his invitation to his audience to join his family 'beside (the) still waters' of the Hawkesbury River.

PSALM 24

IN HEAVEN

Oil on canvas, 243 x 395 cm., (diptych), 1982, Gift of Eileen Chanin and Adrian Morris 1983, Collection of the Art Gallery of New South Wales

'WHO SHALL ASCEND INTO THE HILL OF THE LORD?' (Verse 3) 'HE THAT HATH CLEAN HANDS AND A CLEAN HEART ...' (Verse 4)

Like the previous painting, the setting for this *Psalm* is the Hawkesbury River. A boat full of new arrivals cross the river, now recast as the River Styx, where they are welcomed with flowers by angels, relatives and friends. In the centre of the right hand panel the artist's mother (who has regained her youth) is hugged by her father, next to them a girl cuddles the baby she lost in life and in the far panel a pregnant woman is reunited with the baby she lost in a miscarriage (two very significant events for his mother who also lost children in this way).

In the other panel Christ is shown surrounded by angels reading from the Bible, gathering flowers and blowing a trumpet. Each figure is represented with large hands to greet one another and their fleshy forms and weighty volumes leave us in no doubt about their physical presence in heaven. Like its companion pictures, *Psalms 3, 12* and *15*, the image of heaven Zofrea presents is one of joyous celebration and fecundity. The flowers entwine with the patterns on the clothing and the hills swell and wrap around the figures who mimic their rolling, curvaceous forms. All is at peace. The marriage of humanity with Nature is at the core of the artist's conception of the afterlife and the recurring theme of heaven and resurrection reaffirm his belief in this form of atonement. This painting brings together all those images and ideas from his early visions of life after death and injects a new stability and sense of union. In *Psalms 3* and *15* the figures seem to swirl around the central figure of Christ, as if in a vortex, while the stronger verticals of the figures in this painting mass around each other to form a wedge that pushes Christ and the trumpeting angel toward the top of the hill. It is a monumental composition with all the weight of a great truth.

In many of the paintings in this series the artist's approach is confrontational. He locates individuals within the paintings who stare out at the viewer, inviting their participation or demanding their complicity in the events described. However, in the images of heaven everyone is self-contained, introspective, absorbed in each other or occupied in acts of veneration. The viewer's involvement is limited to that of a detached observer. There is no place for them in heaven until called and while this vision can be a great consolation, it is not an event in which they can become involved. The clarity of Zofrea's vision is what convinces us. Each figure is so precisely drawn and rendered, each flower and blade of grass so sharply outlined that we are encouraged to acknowledge the metaphysical component as an aspect of the everyday.

This absolute clarity and the artist's conviction that the most significant spiritual events are interwoven into the fabric of our lives is as refreshing as it is sustaining.

PSALM 25
Oil on canvas, 183 x 198 cm., 1982

'LOOK UPON MINE AFFLICTION AND MY PAIN ...' Verse 18

The combination of eroticism and indifference recalls Zofrea's illustration of the text 'My God, my God, why hast thou forsaken me?' in *Psalm 22*. Once again the figure of the naked woman emulates Christ's torment on the cross and her naked-ness seems even more exposed because of the indifference of the men playing cards. The suffocatingly claustrophobic space replicates that used in the earlier painting and the young girl's stare is reminiscent of the young man's guilty gaze. Yet despite the similarities it is the differences that are so telling.

The blatant eroticism is modified by the cosy, homely interior and the swirling patterns of clothing, curtains, wallpaper and rugs. Although the men are indifferent to the woman displaying herself in the middle of the room, their lack of concern does not seem to be malicious, just uncaring, and the young girl's expression is full of understanding and inner strength. In fact she is the central character to whom we return continually not only because she addresses us directly, but because of her position as clairvoyant or seer. While the first painting is punitive in its depiction of the men, in this case the artist seems less concerned to apportion blame. The separation of the sexes he describes is merely an extension of the artist's understanding of his Italian heritage, in which the men and women lived very different lives.

Cards are an important image here for although playing cards was a family activity, for the men it was a way of couching their feelings and working out their frustrations and aggressions. It is a surrogate life which Zofrea acknowledges through his image of the young boy building a house of cards. Its frail structure, in imminent danger of collapse, is employed as a metaphor for the lack of substance and escapism he associates with this activity. The women on the other hand are strong, nurturing, erotic and all knowing. It is they who orchestrate the room, even though the presence of the men at the back of the room is given great pictorial weight.

While blame is not apportioned there is the gnawing suspicion that the naked woman may be admiring herself in the mirror and as John Berger[1] has pointed out this is a well established technique for charging women with the responsibility of men's lust, however it is a position he modifies through the comparison he draws between the woman and the Grunewald painting of Christ on the cross. The complexity of these images reinforces his belief that it is extremely difficult to judge another. One reading may be more appropriate, depending on the context, but it is neither right nor wrong.

1.   John Berger, *Ways of Seeing*, Pelican, London, 1972. p. 51.

PSALM 26

(LOREN)
Oil on canvas, 153 x 168 cm., 1982

'I WILL WASH MINE HANDS IN INNOCENCE; SO WILL I COMPASS THINE ALTAR ...'
Verse 6

In both *Psalm 25* and *Psalm 26* Loren makes direct contact with us across a chasm of silence. Her gaze is penetrating, cutting away all artifice and offering a clarity of vision that presupposes some clairvoyant ability. It is a deeply moving painting which eschews many of the devices the artist most often employs to carry his meanings. There is no hint of sound or movement, the space is expansive and unimpaired, one figure interacts solely with us on a very intimate level. It is the antithesis of the great monumental compositions, swelling with people and energy.

What Zofrea achieves in this painting is a quiet, unassuming realism. The immediacy of his vision and his lack of sentiment contribute to this sense of the commonplace, yet the very emptiness of the field and the extraordinarily invasive gaze of the young girl injects an element of mystery that runs just below the surface of this familiarity. His rendering of the minutiae of each blade of grass and his depiction of the cultivated landscape as eerily unpopulated recalls the desolate, lonely paintings of New England by Andrew Wyeth. Indeed the unsettling presence of the woman in one of Wyeth's most famous paintings *Christina's World* is similar in its compositional organisation and emotional intensity to this painting of Loren. The important difference is that Loren is not entirely alone; next to her is a chair about to be filled. Even the choice of deckchairs implies a casualness that seems to override the initial reading of loneliness and desperation. The self confident, all knowing young girl is isolated in a sea of grass that flows up to other houses on the hills around Kurrajong, but it is not a threatening environment and the bright blue deckchairs are set there for a reason. Loren may even be inviting the viewer to join her. If so it would not be unlike Zofrea to lure his audience into his paintings and to encourage his viewers to involve themselves in the action described. It is one of the most compelling devices he uses and Loren is one of his most successful mediums. In *Psalm 25* she dominates the composition of ten figures (including the image of Christ in the painting on the wall) just as she assumes a towering presence in this *Psalm*.

The text he illustrates acknowledges her innocence and accompanies this with her readiness to be tested 'Examine me O Lord, and prove me ...' *Verse 2*. Many are tested in Zofrea's paintings of the Psalms and many are found wanting, but in this case he elevates Loren to a position of spiritual wholeness and worthiness that enables her to face any test with confidence.

PSALM 27

FROM ST PAUL'S LETTERS TO THE CORINTHIANS
Oil on canvas, 90 x 120 cm., 1977

'WAIT ON THE LORD: BE OF GOOD COURAGE, AND HE SHALL STRENGTHEN THINE HEART ...' Verse 14

The family gathering at meal times is one of the most important events in any peasant community. It is not only linked to physical sustenance it is also a moment of spiritual reflection. An important aspect of the meal Zofrea describes in this painting is the dedication of the food to God and the thanksgiving that accompanies its consumption. Farming communities plant and harvest according to the phases of the moon and as the lunar calendar also dictates Saint's days and Christian holidays, the daily experience of attending Mass or consulting the Bible becomes an integral part of life.

This painting is a translation of a photograph of Russian peasants by Robert Capa, which originally appeared in *Ladies' Home Journal*. The image had a deep resonance for the artist who had no difficulty converting the characters to Calabrian peasants dressed in patterned fabrics and sitting at a red and white checked tablecloth. The most immediate art historical reference is to van Gogh's *The Potato-eaters*, that group of humble peasants sitting around their frugal repast under the glow of one weak lamp, their weathered faces and gnarled hands resembling the food they eat. This may well have been an influence on Capa when he took the photograph and its message of honesty and humble toil was not lost on either of the two artists.

Van Gogh, in a letter to his brother Theo described the peasants in his painting as having '... dug the earth with those very hands they put in the dish, and so', he continued 'it speaks of manual labour, and how they have honestly earned their food'[1]. The hands and faces in this *Psalm* tell a similar message of honest toil and belief in God. In particular the woman on the right of the painting holding up her hand in supplication or benediction has all the power and presence of a great religious personage. The size and weight of that arm is awesome, not only as a physical presence but also as a signifier of hard labour. She exudes a confidence and commitment that draws the composition together and injects a further note of instruction. The child is being initiated into the spiritual life of the family through the simple act of eating.

Of course, the central message of The Last Supper is embodied in this painting as it is in all meals for Catholics. Christ as the bread of life is an extremely important image and this family gathering is another way of acknowledging the importance of Christian belief in living a full and nourishing life.

1. Vincent van Gogh, letter to Theo, no. 404, 20 April 1885.

PSALM 28

Oil on canvas, 153 x 168 cm., 1982

'DRAW ME NOT AWAY WITH THE WICKED, AND WITH THE WORKERS OF
INIQUITY …' Verse 3

Zofrea's direct comparison between the imagery of religious paintings, included within his pictures, and the action of the figures in the foreground is a highly provocative pictorial device. It works with dramatic effect in *Psalm 22* and *Psalm 25* when he contrasts the image of a naked woman with the suffering of Christ and in this painting the direct comparison between the image of the Virgin surrounded by the apostles at Pentecost and the scantily clad girl being scrutinised by the men, in what appears to be a bordello, is equally shocking. Or is this a translation of that Biblical story into a suburban house in Sydney? This ambiguity creates a considerable tension which gives the painting a much greater presence than if it were a straightforward contemporary relocation of a Biblical story.

Are the men venerating her or lasciviously summing her up? There is enough visual evidence to support both interpretations, however it is the strong message of the Psalm 'Draw me not away with the wicked', that suggests the more sinister reading. The plush red seats, patterned wallpaper and dark ambience lit by an internal light source are reminiscent of the bordello in *Psalm 14 — Que Dice Donna, Dice Donna*, and her awkwardness seems to demand our sympathy. The posture she adopts while clutching at her stockings and her downcast expression is not the attitude of someone receiving supplicants.

In her essay on the artist, Anna Waldmann points out that the men are positioned '… on three levels, superimposing their flat and strongly coloured shapes in an archaic frieze from which the white and pink body of the woman emerges like a flower's pistil'[1]. This association with the female organ of the flower further reinforces the suppressed sexuality which underlies this group of paintings. Sexuality is a force that is present in all Zofrea's paintings and its relation to his conception of religion is a complex amalgam of grass roots Catholicism and late twentieth century libertarianism. Sex is seen as the natural right of human beings and the source of their greatest pleasure as well as their nadir. While the home may be the shrine of human loving, the bordello is seen as the setting for men and women's degradation.

Within this simplistic outline are many subtleties which Zofrea highlights in different work. In this painting the text indicates that the girl is seeking protection from the lecherous men surrounding her and certainly her demeanour supports this reading. The way in which they press in around her, creating an extremely claustrophobic space, is very threatening and their combined presence acts as a form of cage to hold her firmly in the centre of the composition. Only some divine power, represented by the icons and other religious paintings on the wall offer the hope of salvation.

1.   Anna Waldmann and Stephanie Claire, *Salvatore Zofrea*, p. 104.

PSALM 29

IL SOGNO
Oil on canvas, 150 x 165 cm., 1987

'THE LORD WILL GIVE STRENGTH UNTO HIS PEOPLE; THE LORD WILL BLESS HIS PEOPLE WITH PEACE.' Verse 11

The image of a peaceable kingdom in which all creatures live in harmony with one another is based on a prophecy from *Isaiah 11*, 'The wolf also shall dwell with the lamb, and the leopard shall lie down with the kid ...'. To this Zofrea has added the underlying sexuality of a horned animal, a naked woman and an image of death. The arum lilies and the stand of darkly threatening trees in the background suggest that God will give peace in death while the horned deer replaces the more traditional image of the unicorn as an image of sexual potency.

The recumbent woman exposes her body to the viewer in a manner now familiar through the exploitation of the female body over the past five hundred years. She is asleep and dreaming (the dream of the title). Is it one of sexual fulfillment? The presence of the horned animal staring at her genitals suggests as much and the artist has painted her with an expression that could confirm that reading. As with all the *Psalms* there is a degree of ambiguity, yet while we may be seduced into accepting the notion of a peaceable kingdom in our lives, the message of the dream suggests that this kingdom will only be found in death, and through giving oneself to God.

The ambience of a dream-like state is developed through the artist's use of highly pitched colours, applied in most cases without regard for local colour. Like Chagall and the Norwegian painter Edvard Munch, Zofrea has chosen a palette that implies another state while maintaining links with the everyday world we inhabit. In particular the swirling trees have the character of one of Munch's dream landscapes and the intense colour of the red and yellow deer, standing on the vibrantly green grass, recalls the startling colour combinations of Chagall's later paintings. Only the woman, who is conjuring up this dream, is unaffected by the distortions of colour and form. She remains the hub of the entire event without being entirely caught up in its momentum.

The reflective mood of the painting and its theme of peace in death was, in part, a response to the death of his father in December of the previous year. It was he asserts '... a time of mourning and readjustment'. As we have seen death and the eventual peace to be found in heaven are recurring themes in his *Psalms*. Indeed his confrontation with death after a serious illness was the impetus for the project and his mother's death in 1976 followed by his father's death ten years later were the pivotal events around which he based his interpretation of the individual Psalms.

Not surprisingly then, he focuses on the concept of atonement in a heaven described in *Revelations* as '... this land of peace, where there are no more tears and no more pain'. It is a reassuring image in a world of pain and suffering.

PSALM 30

ROSA
Oil on canvas, 120 x 150 cm., 1987

'FOR HIS ANGER ENDURETH BUT A MOMENT ... BUT JOY COMETH IN THE MORNING.' Verse 5

Sexuality is an ever present concern in Zofrea's painting but few of his pictures match this *Psalm* in its exuberant celebration of human intimacy. Everything he has included, and all the associations he expects us to make about these objects, are carefully contrived to read as an erotic encounter of the most flamboyant and enjoyable kind. It is a riot of physicality and sensuality, exemplified in the unaffected pleasure of their roll in the grass. The thick, fleshy thighs of Rosa's *beau* and her own ample limbs are painted with relish and the none too delicate contact between the couple seems to resound through the picture.

Rosa is one of the few paintings in which there is any real contact with the imagery and pictorial invention of the Colombian artist Fernando Botero. His inflated figures swell at the groin and breasts with such an exaggerated pressure that you find yourself willing them not to burst. Their touch is so heavy and Botero's obvious delight in their fleshy vulnerability so palpable, that it is difficult to look at them without feeling like a voyeur. Rosa and her mate generate a similar awkwardness as they grope away at each other, completely oblivious of our presence.

The artist's interpretation of this *Psalm* is ribald, to say the least. The innuendo apparent in his choice of the lines '... joy cometh in the morning' is quite blatant and the selection of apples and bananas for the fruit basket and a hotdog as the picnic delicacy are further examples of the artist's unrestrained pleasure in the erotic possibilities of this coupling. The couple lie diagonally across the picture leaving very little of the canvas unaffected by their presence and causing the viewer to tumble along with them.

In many of Zofrea's paintings at least one of the figures looks out at us demanding our attention, but in this picture the protagonists are so involved in their own pleasure that they are completely unaware of being observed. As the man lifts his dimpled thigh over his lover the viewer must either involve themselves or look away. Either way, they become involved whether they like it or not and the artist has once again drawn them into his personal narrative and made it an extension of their own lives.

This couple, sighted at Sydney's Clontarf beach in the 1970s, made such an impression on the artist that he revived it ten years later as an illustration to a Psalm whose central message is one of stoicism. That message has been largely ignored however, and Zofrea has converted it into an image of lust and sexual fulfillment.

PSALM 31

DEATH AND TRANSFIGURATION
Oil on canvas, 300 x 195 cm., 1987

'HAVE MERCY UPON ME, O LORD ... MINE EYE IS CONSUMED WITH GRIEF, YEA, MY
SOUL AND MY BELLY.' Verse 9

The busker in Florence, which the artist encountered while on his Churchill
Fellowship studying fresco technique, was the impetus for the imagery employed
in six of the *Psalms*; *Psalms 19–21*, this painting and *Psalms 33* and *34*. Each deals
with the central idea of life as a series of hoops and trials which human beings
encounter in their time on earth.

This painting is a straightforward narrative which is given great poignancy
and weight by the death of the artist's father in 1986. *Death and Transfiguration* is
the most direct in its references to those sources for it depicts the artist's father
lying on his death bed, surrounded by the young busker, his menagerie of trained
animals and his odd assortment of swings, hoops and props. Through his own grief
Zofrea sees his father transformed into a young man once again, climbing the
ladder to heaven and caught between the temporal world he is departing and the
spiritual world he is entering.

Heaven is indicated by the blue sky and the lights strung across the top of the
picture. It is a symbol for the celestial sphere that recurs throughout this series of
works. Another is the ladder, symbolising the course of a life with its eventual
resurrection in heaven. The ladder runs off this painting at the top and the
bottom indicating that it has no beginning and no end. Death and transfiguration
in heaven is one of the most important themes the artist elicits from the first fifty
Psalms and although it is expressed in many ways these images of his father's death
are some of the most moving.

The split between the temporal and the spiritual worlds is a hard and fast
line. Below the line the canvas is cluttered with the trials and tribulations of existence and with such worldly possessions as the old man's watch and playing cards,
the black crow that appeared at his funeral and then flew away as the hearse
left the church, the fallen net which once kept him up and the drum announcing
his death. In Italy the kettle drum is associated with death and is often used
during Easter celebrations when villagers follow the image of the Virgin around
the town helping her to seek out her dead son. One important element is the
repetition of the string of lights that act as a sustaining image of his father's belief
in the resurrection.

The curtain is about to close on one part of his life, and the animals are in confusion as they leap headlong around the picture, but his spirit, reborn as a young
harlequin, has already advanced well up the ladder and is just about to enter the
celestial sphere. This optimism is echoed in the choice of bright colours and the
clear definition of each of the forms. Although he was experiencing an intensely
felt grief after his father's death, the notion of transfiguration is presented with
such clarity that the artist convinces us that his faith sustained him through this
difficult period.

PSALM 32

THE CAROUSEL
Oil on canvas, 225 x 195 cm., 1987

'BE YE NOT AS THE HORSE, OR AS THE MULE, WHICH HAVE NO
UNDERSTANDING …' Verse 9

While in Florence in 1986, Zofrea saw the magnificent *Battle of San Romano* by
Paolo Uccello in the Uffizi. It is one of the great images of the early Renaissance
because it brings together the harmony and precision of the new interest in
mathematics and linear perspective, with a clarity of form and a lively and
inventive use of colour. Coincidentally these are all features that the artist was
exploring in his series based on the busker he had encountered outside the gallery
one day. Bringing the two together was a natural process.

From 1456–57, Uccello painted three versions of the famous battle of 1432
between the victorious Florentines and the Sienese, so after completing this first
exploration of the connotative possibilities of this subject, Zofrea decided to
emulate his feat and base three *Psalms* on the Uffizi picture and its companions
which now hang in the Louvre and the National Gallery in London (*Psalms 35, 37*
and *44*).

Uccello's dumpy horses, frozen in a rearing position, look very much like
carousel ponies spinning endlessly on a circuitous journey and the upright lances
that seem to prop up the horses are reminiscent of the brightly painted poles that
support the roof of the merry-go-round. Consequently their transposition to a fair
ground with all of its connotations of frivolity and pleasure was a logical step for the
artist when illustrating the Psalm's theme of independence and the need to take
initiatives in a world of repetitive gestures.

The young man on the white horse is taking up the Psalm's message to be
'… not as the horse, or as the mule' and riding off the carousel to live his own life.
His departure from the routine of the merry-go-round is signalled in true Zofrean
spirit by a trumpet blast from a fellow traveller. The other riders just stare in
disbelief.

While this might be read as an impetuous act fraught with dangers and pit-
falls, the resolute expression of the young man confirms his faith in his own
actions. To reinforce this positive ambience the artist has set him on the same
horse ridden by the successful armour-clad knight in the far left hand corner of the
Uccello painting. That knight has just felled his opponent and we are encouraged
to believe that our hero will do the same. To underscore the necessity for his
actions the other participants have been mounted on horses whose original riders
were all felled in the Uccello.

The clarity of the formal arrangement of each element in the composition
and the sharp bright colouration evoke memories of childhood, when everything seemed so crisp and clear. A time when the world was full of possibilities
because distinctions between right and wrong weren't blurred by experience.
Unfortunately, we now know that absolute certainty is only a relic of our youthful
innocence.

PSALM 33

IL CIRCO DEL MARE
Oil on canvas, 195 x 225 cm., 1987

'THE LORD BRINGETH THE COUNSEL OF THE HEATHEN TO NOUGHT: HE MAKETH THE DEVICES OF THE PEOPLE OF NONE EFFECT.' Verse 10

In this *Psalm* the busker from Florence and his props have been transported to the seaside, where he waits to perform before the crowds of summer tourists. The animals are ready, the hoops and hurdles are all set in place and the audience are caught up in that moment of silence before things happen. The young man will soon play his saxophone to announce his troupe and the painful trials of life will begin.

After the image of *Death and Transfiguration* in *Psalm 31* Zofrea has returned to the moment before that temporal tightrope walking to examine the superstructure of the game of life. The death of his father and his own illness had confirmed his belief in the transitory nature of human existence and in this painting he is once again seeking an answer to the great question of 'What are we doing here?'. His use of the busker's performance as a metaphor for life indicates the anguish and frustration he was feeling at the time and illustrates his conviction that, though humanity may face the trials and tribulations placed before them, the promise of salvation is ever present.

Once again the lights at the top of the composition symbolise heaven and the ladder standing to one side indicates a means of reaching that goal. Unlike *Psalms 31* and *34*, however, the ladder is shown as having both a beginning and an end; it is not infinite but the span of a life, with very clear demarcations. Just as the sound of the saxophone will herald this performance, so life too has an opening act that is announced with the sound of a baby crying. After the performance the actors leave the stage and in Zofrea's imagery, they ascend to the celestial sphere of the party lights by climbing the ladder. In between anguish and pain must be endured.

At first sight the riot of bright colour seems to deny the anger and frustration implicit in the artist's interpretation of the Psalms, their garish fair ground joviality strikes entirely the wrong note. Nevertheless, it is precisely this reference to the circus that carries his message, for the image of the clown masking his true feelings behind a huge painted grin invokes the metaphor of the circus performance as an endlessly repetitive trial.

At this point in his life the artist was, not surprisingly, convinced of the continuous sadness of life and the need to endure its vicissitudes. This belief is given visual form in the image of the animals about to begin their trials. They represent all humanity although, as the selection of verse in the text implies, it will all go wrong if they don't trust in God.

The areas of flatly applied, bright colour serve to separate each element of the composition and heighten the sense of disjunction between them. The combined effect is a jarring clash of imagery and colour that gives form to the artist's conception of the turmoil and pain of life.

PSALM 34

I GIORNI SONO CONTATI
Oil on canvas, 225 x 195 cm., 1987

'THE LORD REDEEMETH THE SOUL OF HIS SERVANTS: AND NONE OF THEM THAT TRUST IN HIM SHALL BE DESOLATE.' Verse 22

In all of the previous *Psalms* based on the image of the busker the paintings are conceived as a shallow stage-set into which his props have been placed. The viewers are distanced from the action and remain resolutely in their seats observing the performance. With this painting that convention has been ruptured by the selection of multiple viewpoints and the lack of any suggestion of a stage. The artist has chosen to look down on the spinning wheel from an elevated position while the busker and his props are viewed at eye level. It is a device that suggests that he expects his audience to be more closely involved in the action of the *Psalm*.

At a time of crisis when his emotions were whirling around like the spinning wheel in the painting, he also chose colours that reflected the intensity of his thoughts and feelings on the death of his father the previous year. The crisp outlines of each form and the unmodulated application of paint were inspired in part by the early Renaissance artists of the *quattrocento* and also by his recent experience of the light in Italy, that was so incredibly intense that it leeched away modulations of tone.

These formal ideas grew out of the need to depict an internal anger and frustration, however, the overriding belief in the redemption promised in this verse of the Psalm gives the painting a celebratory feeling. It is a tumbling set of images and ideas, accompanied by the shrill tones of the trumpet played by the character on the left of the painting, that involves the viewer in a roller-coaster ride around the canvas.

Fernand Leger's great, late career, figure compositions based on the subject of *La Grande Parade*, are the pictorial models for his new conception of space in which elements are superimposed in a layered collage of ideas. The celestial lights from the earlier paintings in this series are caught up in the swirling movement of the carousel and dragged throughout the painting in scalloping rhythms, while the busker's props are laid over the top as a kind of grid. The young man is ascending the ladder (without a beginning or end) to heavenly redemption. The parrot hanging upside down in a hoop is one of Zofrea's favourite symbols for turmoil and the cat about to leap through another hoop continues the theme of cruelty and pathos associated with the image of the busker and his menagerie.

The image of the busker enables Zofrea to key into one of the most telling of his formative experiences. As a child in Borgia, he remembers Saint's days as the cause of much celebration when visiting circuses or travelling fairs would set up in the village. This conjunction of the fairground with the church, of entertainment and frivolity with deeply held beliefs, is at the root of his narrative technique in this group of pictures and it accounts for their particular resonance.

PSALM 35

AFTER UCCELLO
Oil on canvas, 198 x 300 cm., 1988

'PLEAD MY CAUSE, O LORD, WITH THEM THAT STRIVE WITH ME; FIGHT AGAINST THEM THAT FIGHT AGAINST ME.' Verse 1

Paolo Uccello's series of paintings based on the Battle of San Romano, painted between 1456–57, provided the model for three *Psalms* that deal with the theme of the battle. In this case not an outward battle with 'those that persecute me' (*Verse 3*) but an inner struggle with the vicissitudes of fate. Years of illness had left the artist with ongoing infirmities after a recurrence of fibrosis and this had engendered doubts and frustrations concerning each human being's transient presence on earth.

While studying fresco techniques with Leonetto Tintori in Tuscany in 1986, Zofrea had visited the Uffizi on many occasions to see the version of Uccello's painting that he used as the model for this *Psalm*. In fact Tintori had been involved in the restoration of the painting so even though he already knew it well from reproductions Zofrea became very familiar with the details of this marvellous work.

As he studied the painting the crisp outline of the forms, the play between areas of strong colour and the patterning of the lances and the landscape conjured up associations with brightly coloured and patterned merry-go-rounds he had seen in fairgrounds. This connection to the circus imagery of the busker series was a catalyst that enabled him to develop his ideas about the parallel realities of religion and the fairground. From the early experiences of feast days in Borgia he understood that the pathos of life is acted out and perhaps even exorcised in the bathos of the clown's performance. The endless repetition of these events also seems to mirror humanity's inability to learn from past experiences. Uccello's landscape is therefore depicted as a carousel on which the knights, seated on their stiff 'wooden' horses, are condemned to play out their game of war over and over again.

This notion of a game is emphasised by the addition of a pack of Italian playing cards that feature images of war in highly decorative and stylised illustrations. Ironically these familiar images from the cards also echo Uccello's figures. The card game is a gamble, a competition — not the real thing but a surrogate battle and one the players are seduced into playing over and over again. So just as the dog chasing one rabbit and pursued by another in Uccello's painting has become a painted feature on the carousel and hence condemned to chase its quarry for all eternity without success, so humanity must continue to search out the meaning of life. The only difference in Zofrea's theology is that Christianity does provide a final solution to the pain and suffering encountered. In heaven these questions are finally answered and the promise of that peace drives us on in this life.

PSALM 36
Watercolour, 48 x 60 cm., 1988

'HE DEVISETH MISCHIEF UPON HIS BED; HE SETTETH HIMSELF IN A WAY THAT IS
NOT GOOD; HE ABHORETH NOT EVIL.' Verse 4

In this *Psalm* Zofrea returns to the ideas developed in two previous paintings.
Psalms 16 and *25* contrast the innocence of children with the transgressions of
those that surround them. In the first the comparison is depicted as either a
prophecy of what will befall the young boy or a painful memory for the older
woman in the picture. The other painting contrasts the young boy making a house
of cards against the serious gambling of the men at the table. In the foreground the
young girl sitting in the bottom right staring out at the viewer seems to understand
what the implications of this scene are for all of humanity. She is a seer and her
clairvoyance is compared to the woman wearing dark glasses standing to her right,
who sees through veiled lenses.

These two images are clearly very important for the artist because he has
combined aspects of both of them in this continuing exploration of the theme of
transgression from the teachings of God. 'The transgression of the wicked ...'
(*Verse 1*) is depicted as a conjunction of the young couple taking illicit pleasure in
their bodies and the gamblers at the back of the room playing cards. While this may
seem rather prudish, neither of these activities is entirely tainted and the *Psalms* as
a body of work presents a much more complex image of sexuality and gambling
than this painting suggests.

Many of them celebrate sensuality and the joys of the flesh as the apogee of
human experience. Others link the imagery of card playing with the artist's father
and, while they often retain the meanings associated with deceit and insubstantiality that are imbedded in our language, they also suggest a symbolic connection
with masculinity and strength. Children and childhood are often invoked as an
image of purity and in this *Psalm* the artist explains that the young boy is the image
of innocence for whom God's 'righteousness *is* like the great mountains' (*Verse 6*).
This is represented in the painting as an internal light emanating from the boy
which glows out from the surrounding nocturnal scene. The other figures move
slowly around him in this starkly lit interior, casting ominous shadows on the walls.
Zofrea developed the image of the boy from an early photograph of himself
as a page boy at his sister's wedding, so he has cast himself as the innocent in
this spectacle.

Watercolour is a notoriously capricious medium in the hands of an amateur,
but its lightness and delicacy offer great possibilities of nuance and atmosphere.
While recovering from another bout of serious illness in 1988 the artist turned to
the difficult but less physically demanding medium of watercolour to illustrate a
children's book *Three Golden Rainbows* by Stephanie Claire. It also proved to be an
appropriate medium for continuing his illustration of the Psalms and this work was
the result. Although he had used watercolour before to complete studies for
various pictures, this is the only Psalm conceived as a watercolour.

PSALM 37
AFTER UCCELLO II
Oil on canvas, 178 x 306 cm., 1989

'FOR THE ARMS OF THE WICKED SHALL BE BROKEN: BUT THE LORD UPHOLDETH THE RIGHTEOUS.' Verse 17

In the second of his homages to Uccello, Zofrea chose the *Rout of San Romano* hanging in the National Gallery in London. It is a much freer essay on the subject than his first version for although he has retained the major elements of Uccello's masterpiece on the left hand side of his painting, on the right a new set of characters drawn from a book on Etruscan sculpture are cast as the opposing force. The figure with the elaborate turban remains as the hero in both paintings, but in Zofrea's hands he has become a pathetic figure clutching on to his merry-go-round horse and a trumpet with grim determination. Unlike the warrior leading his men into battle in the original, he is reduced to dragging his disfunctional steed, on its clumsy little trolley, into battle against what appear to be strong and well equipped troops.

The choice of the Etruscans as models for these terrifying opponents is very apposite for they were the ancestors of the Florentines whom they must fight in this battle. Just as every child must confront the Oedipal dilemma of killing their own father to achieve independence, so the 'good guys' in white on the left must slay the dark and determined Etruscans on the right. The artist's relationship with his father is the sub-plot of this painting.

The grief arising from his father's death in 1986 had instigated the *Psalms* based on the Florentine busker and the three versions of Uccello's painting, so as a way of introducing his father into the paintings he employed the imagery of the Italian playing cards, which are a recurring leitmotif for the artist's father. They represent an image of distant, powerful masculine authority that, in this painting, has been trampled under foot. The cards replace dead soldiers in Uccello's original.

Zofrea's determination to become an artist was flying in the face of his father's aspirations for his son and the success he achieved was never fully appreciated by his father.[1] So after the grief of his death had abated it was an appropriate time to confront this power struggle and to assert his authority in the medium he had chosen as a battleground. This is not done with total conviction however, and the pack of cards on which the rest of the army stand appears ready to topple over. Nevertheless, the white army spurred on by the trumpet call has God's promise to 'uphold the righteous'.

Elements of the busker's props remain in the foreground of the battle as an indication of the trials humanity must suffer and as a reminder that this is just another of those trials.

1. See Stephanie Claire and Anna Waldmann, *Salvatore Zofrea*, Hale & Iremonger, Sydney, 1983. p. 55. Also in an article in *La Fiamma*, 9 August 1976, the artist describes how his father had thought his wish to be an artist was madness and told his sisters to '... take me and hang me by the feet from the Spit Bridge and shake me until I returned to my senses.'

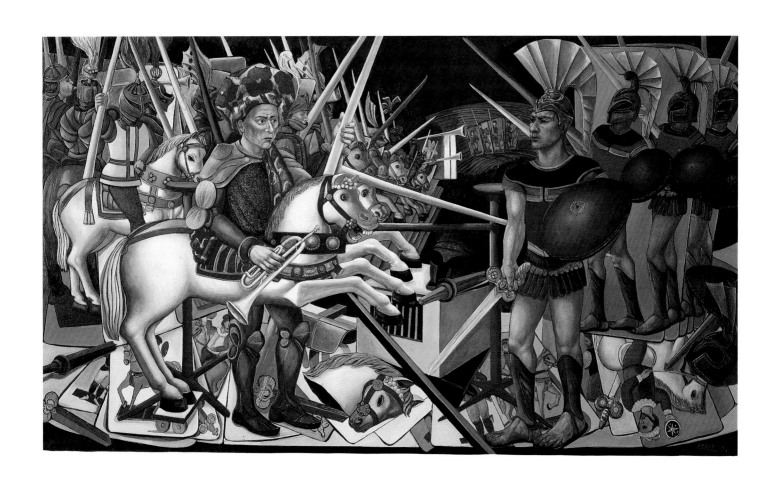

PSALM 38

Oil on canvas, 120 x 180 cm., 1988

'I AM TROUBLED: I AM BOWED DOWN GREATLY: I GO MOURNING ALL THE DAY
LONG.' Verse 6

This quiet and reflective painting comes as quite a surprise after the crowded, claustrophobic spaces of the previous group of *Psalms*. Their jazzy brightness and strident imagery, based on photographs of a busker and his entourage, were the visual manifestation of the artist's anger, fear and frustration after the death of his father and the recurrence of his own illness. The isolation and loneliness described in this *Psalm* is the other dimension of that grief. Indirectly inspired by the mood of so many of Fellini's films in which characters find themselves in desolate summer resorts walking along the beach in the early hours of the morning, or sitting in a cafe with its bamboo blinds crackling in the wind, this painting began from photographs of a similar place at the seaside village of Quercianella in Italy.

The intense loneliness manifested in a place which normally holds crowds of festive patrons is milked to the full by Fellini and Zofrea achieves a similar forlorn environment in this painting. A concurrent influence during the genesis of the painting was a book on the American painter Richard Diebenkorn. One of his paintings from the fifties, *Interior with Book*, is suffused with a blue light that pervades the interior and sweeps out into the sky. It depicts the corner of a room with windows at waist height all around. An empty chair stands in front of a table on which is placed a cup and an open book. In fact it is almost the same scene depicted in the cafe at Quercianella, with the important exception that the figure, often found in Diebenkorn's work from this period, has departed. Whereas the American artist suggests the human drama through the absence of the figure and by investing his own idiosyncrasies of touch and brushwork with all the weight of significance he can conjure up, Zofrea asks us to concentrate on the figure of the woman at the table.

The blue under-painting which he began with in response to the Diebenkorn painting is a pervasive influence throughout the canvas, contributing to the mood of quiet desperation. It is instructive to note how the American's freely painted and scumbled surface, splattered with drips, has been reworked in the manner of another American realist Edward Hopper. Zofrea is interested in the narrative possibilities of the scene and Diebenkorn's delight in the application of paint places too much attention of the surface of the canvas so in this painting the brittle illusion of a deep space, in which the woman's loneliness is made palpable, is more important in his overall scheme and those aspects of the American artist's work had to be repressed.

In an earlier version of the painting a young man sat at the table with the bottle of beer in the foreground, but as the work progressed he distracted from the girl's dilemma. By removing him and suggesting his presence through the empty bottle on the table Zofrea places even greater attention on the forlorn young woman.

PSALM 39

Oil on canvas, 183 x 137 cm., 1978

'LORD, MAKE ME TO KNOW MINE END, AND THE MEASURE OF MY DAYS … THAT I
MAY KNOW HOW FRAIL I AM.' Verse 4

This work was painted ten years earlier than the previous *Psalm*, as a way of dealing with his mother's death. The shock of that event was one of the instigating
forces behind the project of illustrating all of the Psalms and in the images of death
and final resurrection in heaven he found a way of coping with his grief.

Before he began work on this vision of his mother's funeral, Zofrea had
painted an important series based on her life that had won the Sulman Prize in
1977. This group of works and in particular *Woman's Life, Woman's Love II* have all
the painful awkwardness of a posed photograph. The triptych depicts the anxiety
he imagined would accompany an arranged marriage and the eventual ossification
of a relationship that was built on duty not love.

This investigation of his parents' life together enabled him to give expression to what he saw as his mother's trials. Life as a trial followed by redemption
in heaven is the recurring imagery throughout the *Psalms* so once having docu-
mented the frustrations and difficulties of her life the artist chose to record his
mother's funeral. The painting is constructed from a nexus of his experience as an
adult and as a child, looking on at one of the most momentous events in his life.

The young boy (Zofrea himself) sees with the innocence of childhood, not
quite encompassing the full weight of what is happening. Next to him the artist
depicts his suffering as an adult through the image of a kneeling man making a
benediction over his mother's grave. This combination of responses indicates the
artist's own confusion at the time. Indeed the painting does not seem to be sited in
the present but in the past, as if to add to the sense of distance and dislocation. It is
more the young boy's image of the world than the man's, although this is explained
in part by the artist's choice of sources.

The painting is based on the cemetery at French's Forest, Sydney, where his
mother is buried, but the central imagery is translated from a photograph reproduced in a book of American life between 1935–43, *In this Proud Land*. It represents
a family visiting relative's graves in Louisiana in 1938. The migrant experience in
Australia has only begun to find its chroniclers over the past two decades and in
this painting Zofrea not only creates a very poignant image of his own grief on the
death of his mother, but manages to encapsulate the larger issues of displaced
families establishing their roots in the new land through the death and interment
of its members. This idea is given credence by the family members of all ages who
have come to the cemetery. The young boy represents their future, built on the
pain and suffering of the past, and the clarity with which he depicts himself in that
role indicates Zofrea's confidence in that future.

PSALM 40
AFTERNOON AT QUERCIANELLA
Oil on canvas, 195 x 240 cm., 1987

'FOR INNUMERABLE EVILS HAVE COMPASSED ME ABOUT: MINE INIQUITIES HAVE TAKEN HOLD UPON ME, SO THAT I AM NOT ABLE TO LOOK UP ...' Verse 12

Following his return from Italy and his father's death, Zofrea began working on the material he had gathered on his Churchill Fellowship. Included amongst this information was a series of photographs of the seaside town of Quercianella in Tuscany. The interior of a small cafe on the water was the source material for *Psalm 38* and the environment outside the cafe provided the setting for this painting. Only the deckchairs used in both pictures indicate any similarity of origin although both are images of loneliness and isolation.

A stronger connection is to the series of *Psalms* based on the busker which he painted in the same year. The horizontal division into earth and sky is similar to the division into the temporal and spiritual domains described in *Psalm 31*. The row of lights along the front echoes the promise of heaven in the earlier work. Similarities also exist in the clear demarcation of the elements in the picture and the use of symbolism, even though this work employs a more traditional mode of describing space and situating figures in that space. The strong shadows and the downcast expression of the girl inject a note of sadness and forbearance that succinctly illustrates the verse from the Psalm. In the background two deckchairs, that seem to have been only recently vacated, suggest that the girl has been left alone to deal with her problems. Zofrea uses the deckchair throughout the *Psalms* and in other pictures painted around this period because of their ability to accommodate a human being and then to retain the memory of that form. It makes them an ideal metaphor for the presence and absence of individuals. In this case they are drawn into the composition along perspective lines that run off to a vanishing point at the far right of the painting, linking them conclusively to the girl as friends or members of her family that no longer offer companionship or support. Considering that the artist had recently lost his father, the imagery has a very poignant resonance.

As we know from the early *Psalms*, Zofrea's theology acknowledges sin and suffering as an essential condition of humanity. However, the promise of redemption or salvation is always at hand. In this case it is manifested in the row of lights that sit just below the sky and also in the open book on the table next to the girl. The book's pages are blank suggesting a fresh start and the possibility of putting aside the mistakes and suffering of the past. Alongside is a bowl of prime fruit, redolent with the promise of nourishment and potential.

Both this *Psalm* and *Psalm 38* pay homage to the realism of artists such as the American Edward Hopper. His images of urban dislocation and loneliness provide one of the many models for Zofrea's essays on the Psalms.

PSALM 41

Oil on canvas, 150 x 165 cm., 1989

'ALL THAT HATE ME WHISPER TOGETHER AGAINST ME: AGAINST ME DO THEY DEVISE HURT.' Verse 7

After a recurrence of illness in 1988 Zofrea was forced to recuperate for much of the following year. Despite the considerable difficulties this imposed upon him he managed to complete three large canvasses, *Psalm 37 — After Uccello II* and *Psalms 41* and *42*, all of which dealt with the torment of those months. Of the three, this painting is the closest to a self-portrait because it represents the frustration and anxiety of dealing with a painful and debilitating disease. The man slumped in a posture of desperation occupies a room full of images of danger, torture and despair. They are the phantoms of his mind made concrete and allowed to spill out into the small, dark room to torment him. The butchered carcass of a sheep hangs behind the man, a tormented dog lies at his feet and to his right an Etruscan helmet in a cage hangs from a butcher's hook. It is a claustrophobic space that not only contains him but also limits any action. The entrails cascading out of the sheep's carcass are a powerful image of the weakness of the flesh and the inevitability of death. This theme is elaborated through the inclusion of the writhing dog, in what seem to be its death throes, and in the suffering of the central character.

Zofrea establishes a narrative sequence of life and death that links the dead sheep, the dying dog and the man. Is the man responsible for butchering the sheep and strangling the dog? To what degree are human beings responsible for the problems that befall them? While the text of the Psalm is rather punitive in seeking revenge on those that seek to hurt or undermine one another, Zofrea's image suggests that humans play their own cards. Fate may determine the cards dealt but individuals make choices that affect their lives. The Italian playing cards certainly suggest such a reading. Within the midst of this despair and chaos one candle lights the room and a golden ladder leans against the wall.

As usual in his paintings, Zofrea counters despair with hope, in this case the candle which is both a symbol of faith and, more importantly, of the presence of Christ. So despite the image of desolation the artist confirms his faith that belief in Christ can provide a way out. Indeed the intensity of the light emanating from the tiny candle and its strength against the dull light of evening entering from the window are indications of its prominence in the artist's life. Escape is given visible form in the image of the golden ladder, even though it is clearly not an easy option because some of the rungs are missing. Nevertheless, the possibility of redemption in heaven is an essential component of Zofrea's theology.

All these ideas are brought together with precision as each form is given its own weight in the composition and those that demand more of our attention are painted in pure colour pitched at a very high key. It is this theatrical intensity that gives the image its commanding presence.

Psalm 42

Oil on canvas, 150 x 165 cm., 1989

'My tears have been my meat day and night, while they continually say unto me, Where is thy God?' Verse 3

The battle between men and women is a recurring theme in Zofrea's work. In the pictures depicting family life it is represented as a division of roles that imposes a physical separation on the participants, and in the bordello images as exploitation. *Psalm 42* introduces another variant, the woman as aggressor, embodied in the form of a two headed, bare breasted bird of prey who assaults the man lying prone along the bottom of the canvas.

Man is represented as a victim of his own sexual desires from his youth to old age. Only in childhood is he innocent and able to confront the world openly. The young man naked in the foreground is trapped by desire, his legs bound as he shields himself from his own innocence with a gesture of dejected embarrassment while the active two-headed female eagle attacks his flesh. Later as an old man he is still caged by his desires and ensnared by the endless serpent of the passions that continue to torment him. The imagery is obvious and the meaning unequivocal.

The woman grooming herself to the right of the picture looks on disinterestedly, unconcerned or perhaps unaware of her role in this painful and bizarre performance. Sexuality is a dominant force in all of Zofrea's work although it is rarely treated as honestly or painfully. It is the 'sword in my bones' (*Verse 10*) given visual form in the image of an Italian playing card inflated to gigantic proportions which acts as a bed for the young man.

For Zofrea the image of redemption is once again evoked in the row of lights that run along the top of the painting. This is the tangible presence of God's promised release from the torments of the physical world. In the previous *Psalm* the artist presented this as a very available means of escape in the form of a ladder. However, there is no escape from sexual desire and within the artist's philosophy men are condemned to suffer without hope of a reprieve until their death. The desperation of this situation is reinforced by the confinement of the room and the cropping of the figures at either side of the composition.

Claustrophobic spaces which offer no escape are common settings in Zofrea's paintings because they compress the action and heighten the sense of theatricality. They are like small stages, overflowing with actors and dramatically lit from unseen spots. The very frontal orientation of this composition gives an even stronger sense of a proscenium arch separating the viewer from the action they are witnessing. The viewer here is only permitted to be an audience not a participant, even though the eyes of the young boy seem to demand sympathy, however, his presence is also ambiguous because he is based on a photograph of the artist as a page boy, implying that it is the artist pondering his own sexuality.

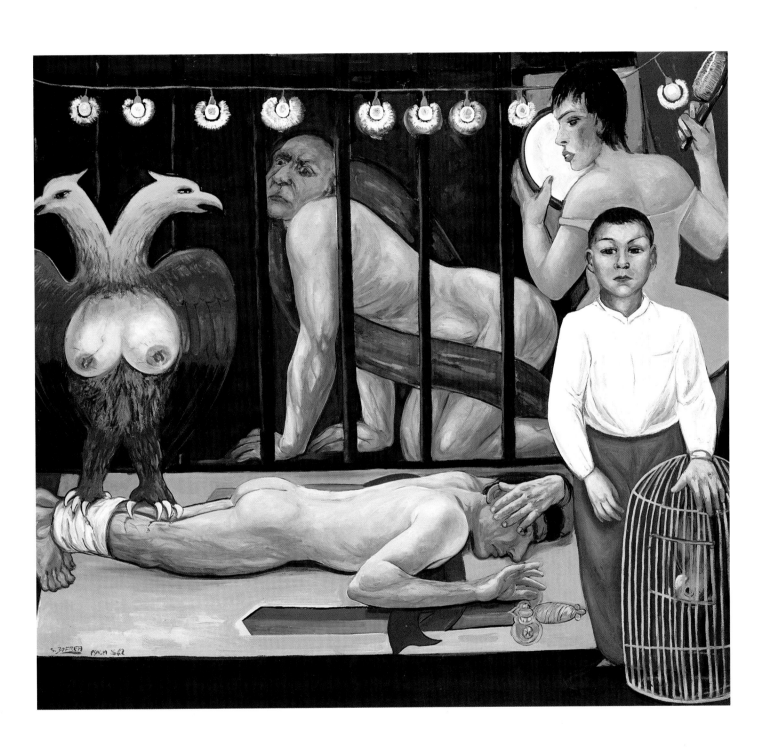

PSALM 43

Oil on canvas, 195 x 150 cm., 1989

'... O DELIVER ME FROM THE DECEITFUL AND UNJUST MAN.' Verse 1

Zofrea was born into a large family in a village in Calabria. As a consequence he finds the image of a small room choked with people of all ages from babies to the elderly a very potent metaphor for family life. Throughout this series of paintings there are numerous images of crowded rooms in which characters act out different dramas while trapped within a claustrophobic space that offers little chance of escape. They are often set at night so that the room becomes an oasis of light in that darkness, protective but ensnaring. Rooms full of different biographies, held together by an unseen controlling structure. A large umbrella of life that represents both the family and the world at large.

In this *Psalm* the central activity is a game of cards, played to the accompaniment of a cornet and overseen by a large woman combing her hair in front of a full length mirror. The game takes on mammoth proportions for the three central players for whom this is much more than a pleasant way to pass time. Indeed one card swells to fill the right hand side of the painting as a symbol of the inflated importance ascribed to the game which can lead to treachery or even death.

The two card players, intensely involved in outsmarting each other, are a straightforward illustration of the first verse of the Psalm. We can assume that their dejected colleague in the foreground has been defeated in the game and whether deceitfully or unjustly, he is now out of the game with a debt to pay.

The image of men playing cards is important to Zofrea because he associates it with masculine bonding. It is a very male activity that not only isolates men from women, but also sets out the parameters of masculine behaviour. He also associates the cards with fate and gambling with choices individuals make in their lives. Cards confer an active involvement with life which is very different from the role assigned to women, who often just stand and preen themselves. However, although this may seem a detached and distanced action, the woman with long hair is active in her own way and, like the card players, a woman at her toilet is a recurring motif in Zofrea's paintings. She is most often introduced as an illustration of how individuals can use physical beauty to manipulate situations to achieve an advantage.

Who needs to be delivered from the deceitful, then? Presumably the young man with his head in his hands, though each of the characters is caught up in a situation that is not completely satisfactory. It is another aspect of the trial of life through which human beings must pass. The only escape in Zofrea's theology is through a belief and trust in God so once again he has strung a row of lights across the back of the composition as a temporal reminder of the spiritual domain that is available to all believers.

PSALM 44

AFTER UCCELLO III
Oil on canvas, 195 x 300 cm., 1990

'THROUGH THEE WILL WE PUSH DOWN OUR ENEMIES: THROUGH THY NAME WILL WE TREAD THEM UNDER THAT RISE UP AGAINST US.' Verse 5

This is the third painting based on Paolo Uccello's series of pictures illustrating the Battle of San Romano. Its source is the painting held in the collection of the Louvre, in Paris. Like the previous pictures he takes the essential composition and structure of the original and introduces ideas and imagery that relate to his current concerns in other *Psalms*, such as the Italian playing cards and the Etruscan sculptures.

Importantly in this work Zofrea has also placed himself at the centre of the conflict, mounted on a white charger and confronting the iniquities that surround him. One of Zofrea's most common devices is to use the setting of the paintings as a metaphor for the central character's mental state. A room, a street, a carousel and in this case a battle are more than the physical setting, they are the personally constructed environments in which we all live. We create our own hells and in this case the image of a battle, in which all the other participants are helmeted and depersonalised, is a very powerful metaphor for the artist's sense of anger and frustration at the world after years of painful and debilitating illness.

Rather than being a self-pitying image it is a celebration of his own strength of character in the face of danger that simultaneously places him firmly within the larger tradition of painting. The choice of Uccello as a guide is both an acknowledgment of his Italian heritage and a reinforcement of his interest in the early Renaissance painters such as Giotto, the Lorenzetti brothers and of course Uccello himself. This Italian lineage goes further back than the fourteenth century, however, and as one way of confirming his own strength he establishes his genealogy back to the Romans and before them to the Etruscans. In this sense the painting is like a family tree sending its roots deep into the rich artistic past of Italy.

To reinforce this, Zofrea has taken great care with the technical construction of the picture. It is a very large canvas, roughly the same size as Uccello's original, and each section was painted to play-off the qualities of the areas that surround it. Some are highly glazed while others are built up texturally to provide contrast and to explore the range of painterly possibilities thrown up by the Renaissance.

Imbued with the confidence of his heritage and with a sharply focused anger the opponents fall down like a pack of cards. This image provides the opportunity to make those same cards into a battle field, after all the Italian cards he uses replicate the heraldry, valor and glory of war in their imagery, and the comparison draws out some interesting connections with earlier *Psalms*. However, the glamour depicted on the cards is only a veneer and in the metaphor of the game Zofrea introduces the recurring image of fate dealing a dreadful hand. The solution is to trust in God, 'For I trust not in my bow, neither shall my sword save me' (*Verse 6*).

PSALM 45
Oil on canvas, 107 x 122 cm., 1991

'THINE ARROWS ARE SHARP IN THE HEART OF THE KING'S ENEMIES ...' (Verse 5).
'THOU LOVEST RIGHTEOUSNESS, AND HATEST WICKEDNESS ...' (Verse 7)

Although the text of *Psalm 45* extols the beauty of women and calls upon them to be dutiful as a preparation for marriage, the artist questions the myths of romantic love associated with this form of patriarchal control. By introducing the figure of the coarse and irrational centaur representing the mind/body split in human beings, he suggests that the woman is a victim of man's animal instincts.

The beast/man is a powerful symbol of aggressive eroticism and in earlier mythology this physical tension between man and animal represented a conflict between good and evil. The tension between righteousness and wickedness, illustrated in this *Psalm*, is another example of Zofrea's exploration of the internalised sexual tension he sees as an inherent part of man's character. The centaur moving forward to embrace the naked woman hunching in a protective foetal position is an interesting variant on the typical representation of the centaur. In Zofrea's bestiary he has a man's front legs and genitals instead of the more usual body of a horse which grows into a male torso at the neck. In this case the hind quarters of a horse grow from his buttocks. Presumably this centaur, with two sets of genitals, has even greater difficulty in containing his sexual desire. To further emphasise the rampant sexuality of the man/beast, he wears a very phallic sword at his waist which points aggressively at the girl.

The mood of the later *Psalms* becomes progressively darker and more ominous as the relationships between the protagonists in the pictures intensifies. In many of the earlier paintings the action hasn't begun and the air is filled with an expectant silence, however in this painting and in several of the later works the performance has already begun and the viewer becomes an unwitting audience to the events described. Like the two witnesses at the back of the stage, the viewer is placed into the iniquitous position of a voyeur or worse still of a disinterested spectator disinclined to be involved.

At the same time the figures are physically more present. The artist achieves this through a greater attention to the details of their musculature and his rendering of the nuances of skin colouration. This has an additional spin-off in that the focus on their weighty fleshiness gives them a greater psychological presence. Paradoxically, although the viewer is drawn physically closer to the actors in these dramas they are given less and less of a role to play.

PSALM 46

Oil on canvas, 150 x 180 cm., 1990

'HE MAKETH WARS TO CEASE UNTO THE END OF THE EARTH; HE BREAKETH THE BOW, AND CUTTETH THE SPEAR IN SUNDER; HE BURNETH THE CHARIOT IN THE FIRE.' Verse 9

In a previous *Psalm* Zofrea represented the state of his own mind as a battlefield and placed the action within that encompassing idea to give weight to his conviction that life is a series of conflicts. This painting is based on a similar premise, the deserted street at night is used as a metaphor for the young man's loneliness and sense of desolation. Night is a symbol of the mysterious dark, the irrational, the unconscious and of course death, and in this picture all those ideas are relevant as indications of the central character's underlying motivations.

Trapped in the dark shroud of his clothes, the man stares out with a plaintive expression, seeking some recognition of his situation from the viewer. In earlier paintings the artist separated his audience from the events he described by setting up a proscenium arch and interposing the conventions of the stage to distance the two. In this painting the viewer is once again placed in the position of an audience. However, it is not the anonymity of the stage that is the structuring device here; instead he chooses the moment when the actor breaks from the action and addresses his audience directly. The actor standing in front of a painted backdrop and flats is about to deliver his soliloquy which will establish a more personal interaction and draw the viewer into a collusive relationship. To emphasise this relationship the viewer is positioned at his eye level to inject a chilling familiarity into the quiet desperation of the scene.

The text Zofrea has chosen to illustrate adds to this ambient discomfort because it suggests the disruption caused by the cessation of hostilities. Although the battle is over, whether won or lost, many problems remain to taunt the survivors. The carousel of life continues to turn. Circus life, merry-go-rounds and the performance of the busker all have a special potency for the artist who sees them as a metaphor for the veneer of everyday life played out by a group of tormented souls putting on a happy face. In this case the carousel, accompanied by a screeching horn, played by a young child wearing an African mask, is a further elaboration of the young man's inner torment about whether to continue to play the game of life.

The destruction promised by the Psalm is depicted in the large image of an Etruscan sculpture of a warrior standing on a flaming chariot. Throughout the later *Psalms* the image of Etruscan soldiers represents the artist's pride in his Italian heritage and the strength this has brought him. At the same time it represents his victory over his ancestors/family which has enabled him to establish his own place in the world. When brought together on the imposing billboard that casts its shadow over the painting, these ideas suggest both the reason for the young man's dejection and a means to confront his desperation.

PSALM 47

Oil on canvas, 120 x 180 cm., 1989

'CLAP YOUR HANDS, ALL YE PEOPLE; SHOUT UNTO GOD WITH THE VOICE OF TRIUMPH.' Verse 1

In the small Calabrian village where Zofrea lived as a child, people would twist their rattles and bang drums as they announced the arrival of Christ into the village during a big parade, then on Sunday it became a more sombre but no less noisy event when the entire village accompanied the Virgin Mary on her search for her lost son. This association of Christ with the village was so deeply ingrained that it seemed natural to him to set this version of the Easter story in Borgia.

Christ enters the village heralded by a man in a horse's costume playing a trumpet and is greeted by a prostitute, as some of the disinterested villagers look on. Zofrea's sense of parody is given full play in his depiction of the donkey perched upon a skateboard. The poor animal can barely hold up this very human Christ, his huge feet poking out in front of the animal as he perches awkwardly on the tiny donkey. The figure preceding them is also a parody of the central figure in *Psalm 37 — After Uccello II*, who leads his army into battle against his own history. It is also a parodic essay on the centaur driven by his physical needs found in *Psalm 45*. At the same time, his choice of this imagery to illustrate the chosen text, '... shout unto God with the voice of triumph', is made with his tongue firmly in his cheek.

Zofrea uses parody as a way of stressing the mockery of Christ and also as a reminder of the possibility of using the most mundane features of our lives as props for deeply felt spiritual events. These are the chinks in the repetitive walls of everyday existence that enable us to encounter the fundamental truths about our lives, just as the lights that hang over the street can be transfigured into an image of heaven in Zofrea's iconography. The simple street scene with its wildly irreverent company of prostitutes, clowns and bored spectators is similarly recast as the site of Christ's entry into Jerusalem. While its significance as an historical event may not be immediately obvious to the villagers on the street, the large Italian playing cards representing kings and military power have been turned upside down by his presence. It is clear that the old order has been changed irreversibly.

This scene is viewed from a street corner where, as a young child, Zofrea might well have watched his family and friends parading at Easter. It is a significant vantage point because the image is conjured up from the child's uninhibited and uncritical experience. The bizarre conjunctions of people and events are seen as commonplace; there is no tendency to romanticise them or make them more important because they are already exciting and interesting to the unselfconscious eyes of a child. Zofrea gives us back this sense of wonder and opens another window in the commonplace of existence.

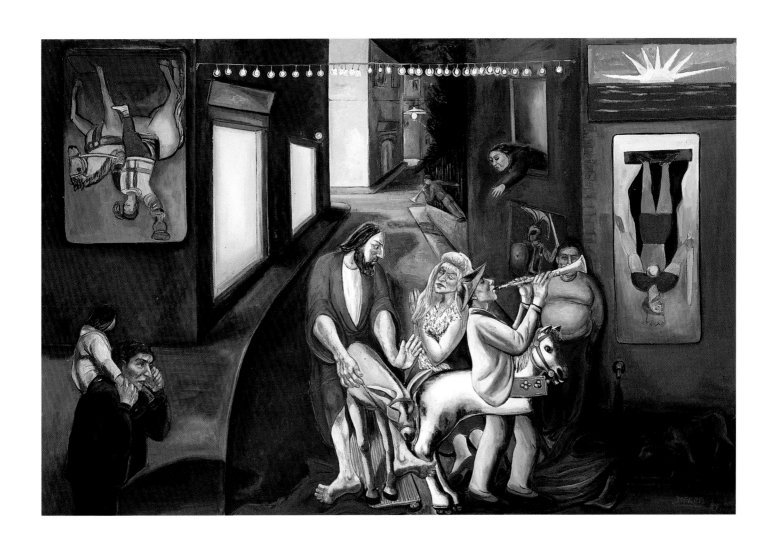

PSALM 48
Oil on canvas, 122 x 107 cm., 1991

'THEY SAW IT, AND SO THEY MARVELLED; THEY WERE TROUBLED, AND HASTED AWAY.' Verse 5

The centaur from *Psalm 45* reappears in this painting as a less aggressive, through equally dangerous presence. The game of seduction he is playing out with the naked woman has a foregone conclusion. His drawn sword and the image of two lovers in the painting on the wall confirm this, as does the horror expressed by the two men playing their own game at the kitchen table.

Games are a recurrent metaphor for life in this series of paintings and the game of love is one of the most common themes. The mind/body split, personified in the physical form of the centaur, is the key to understanding the tensions that underlie this game for Zofrea. In his game plan men are driven by their sexual desire and terrified by its power. The coarse and irrational forces represented by the centaur are unleashed by sexual desire in a Dionysian orgy that the righteous and rational side of his personality cannot control. In horror he must sit to one side and watch as the libido takes over.

In this reading of male sexuality, both men at the table are accepting responsibility for the seduction of the woman and one has even drawn a sword to put an end to it, in fulfilment of *Verse 10*, '... the right hand is full of righteousness.'

Just as the ambience of the later *Psalms* has become darker and more ominous, the space has begun to squeeze in on the figures, forcing them together in a contorted jumble of humanity. The combined effect of these changes is to create a pressure cooker in which human emotion is kept at boiling point. Only the silence and timelessness of the painting acts as a safety valve to keep the drama under control.

Zofrea has developed this approach to picture making over the past few years as a way of exorcising his own devils and also as a means of drawing his audience into a closer relationship with the psychological tensions he depicts. His belief that great art can only emerge from significant physical and emotional experiences is extended into a theory of reception which is based on the ability of individuals to identify their own experiences in those represented in the painting.

The Psalms operate as a trigger for the artist's introspection and the viewer is then reconfirmed in their own beliefs through the veracity of those experiences. 'They can say "I know what it's like for that to happen to me",' explains Zofrea, and because of this connection they transcend the specific events depicted and expand them to embrace a universal truth about existence.

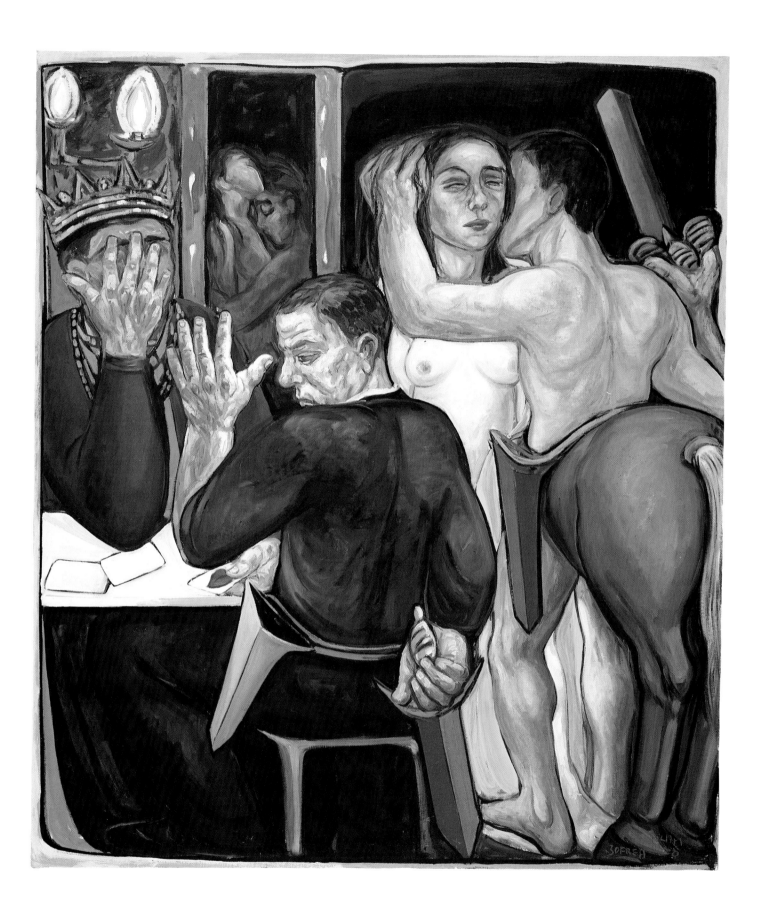

Psalm 49
Oil on canvas, 125 x 180 cm., 1991

'This their way is their folly ...' Verse 13

This *Psalm* is the culmination of the series of pictures based on a busker and his troupe of animals the artist saw in Florence in 1986. The busker's hoops and tightropes form the superstructure around which the composition is built and the cat, who was so tormented in the earlier paintings, now sits calmly on the table after surviving its ordeal. It is the old woman, who stares at the cat with such contempt, who has fared worse. The folly of her life is written in her face. It is a landscape of events in a life that has been wasted. In its wake is only bitterness and disappointment. The most striking difference between this painting and the earlier images of the busker is the dark, foreboding atmosphere which surrounds the figures. In place of the clearly articulated planes of pure colour and the intricate pattern-making that linked human beings with the busker's props there is a strong spotlight on the central figures casting deep shadows and swallowing up colour into a sombre range of dark blues, reds and greens.

This change of mood indicates a move away from the anger of the first images to a more resentful and disillusioned attitude. The old woman clings tenaciously to the trappings of her beauty, but the game is up and she knows it. In front of her a clown occupies a prominent place in the composition. Zofrea often uses the clown as a sinister image, duplicitous and dangerous, suggesting that the old woman has been tricked into giving up her life by others and is now left with nothing to show. It is a reading reinforced by his use of another recurring motif, the parrot hanging upside down in a cage, which appears in many of the *Psalms* to indicate the tragicomedy of life. The young man wearing white gloves is also cast as a harbinger of danger. He is the embodiment of deceit.

This strange group of characters are sitting on the water's edge at night just as a storm is about to break. As in most of the later *Psalms* the environment in which the protagonists stand is a crucial indication of their mental state, and in this case the brewing storm is a very powerful metaphor for their bitterness and malevolence. The only sign of hope is the brittle joviality of the row of party lights that hangs above their heads. In many of the paintings from the busker series this is used as a symbol of heaven, and once again it is presented as a promise of salvation and the final solution to all temporal problems.

Coming to the end of the trials and tribulations of her life, embodied in the busker's props at the back of the group, the central dissolute female character is offered spiritual redemption. Although the narrative is more pessimistic, the moral is the same as that presented in the other paintings influenced by the performance of the busker.

PSALM 50
Oil on canvas, 120 x 180 cm., 1991

'THOU GIVEST THY MOUTH TO EVIL, AND THY TONGUE FRAMETH DECEIT.' Verse 19

The couple sitting at this small table playing out the game of life are trapped in the vice of their past. Two screen-like cards push in on them, bringing back the memories of past events responsible for the rupture that now exists. Zofrea often uses cards as a metaphor for life and as a way of describing the surrogate relationships that can replace intimacy.

Throughout the *Psalms*, card players are often juxtaposed against lovers to contrast the familiarity of mates with the joys and the dangers of sexuality and to emphasise the notion that life is a game in which each move has a consequence. Of course it also suggests that life is a gamble and raises the possibility of stacked decks, bad hands and cheating. Seen in this light, the couple at the table playing out an intimate relationship through the surrogate replacement of a disconsolate game of cards are separated by the experiences of life. The sexual encounters that fill the starkly lit room are memories of their own intimacy or perhaps reminders of their past indiscretions as suggested by the text '... and has been partaker with adulterers.' (*Verse 18*).

The young couple, embracing as they dance, appear in two previous painting (*Psalms 16* and *36*) that also include a young boy and an old woman to indicate the state of innocence before sexual encounter and its consequences. Also included in the second of these paintings is a group of card players sitting at the back ignoring the events surrounding them. This game of life is most often played at night in a domestic interior in which the trappings of everyday life become threatening props and it is most often played by men because of the important association the artist makes with his family's interest in cards. In this painting, however, the chaos caused by passion is visited upon a couple caught in the middle of these events. The man is disillusioned and despondent, his partner confused and seeking assurance from outside. Their torment not only registers in the intensity of their expressions, it fills the space around them and is given poignant weight in the clumsy awkwardness of their fleshy hands.

The sharp contrasts of red, green and yellow filling the background of the painting introduce an acidic edge to the composition that pushes the two card players closer toward us until they are barely contained by the edge of the canvas and their torment is made uncomfortably present. The distance between them is marked by an image of a disdainful naked woman being passionately caressed by a suppliant man. This blurred first embrace leads inexorably to the betrayal and finally the separation of the two.

Whether the central lovers represent the couple or the man and his mistress is unclear but what is certain is that sexual passion which brought them together is now responsible for their separation.

Salvatore Zofrea (right) talking with Ted Snell (Photograph: Willie Mobbs)

AN INTERVIEW WITH SALVATORE ZOFREA
Ted Snell: Kurrajong and Greenwich NSW, 12 February 1990

Why did you decide to paint the entire one hundred and fifty Psalms?

That was the pledge I made after my experience of being sick, of being really sick in hospital in 1975. It really had an impact on me. Discovering the Psalms made it fit together and when I was recovering and able to work again, I saw it as God saying to me get on with some serious painting, some serious images, instead of the trivial, superficial pastiche I was doing. So I want to get the whole bloody lot done.

What was your inspiration for working on the Psalms?

I think that it was just due to the fact that I had the experience of being ill and close to death. That's how I discovered the Psalms. I never knew they existed until I was about 28 and in hospital and a friend of mine said to me, 'Have you read the Psalms?'. So she introduced me to them and I read them in a state of anxiety because I was really conscious of how sick I was. Under the great threat of dying I became aware of my surroundings and the superficial life I had been living.

That's why, before I took notice of all of these different emotions in me, I was drawn to a type of painting which was more physically appealing, like the Expressionists and van Gogh. I saw their exuberant, impulsive mood and because I didn't need to look too deeply within myself, that type of painting was very attractive to me.

What was your intention when you began interpreting the Psalms?

Before I actually experienced physical pain through illness I had gone through a crisis when I had rejected the Christian faith and Catholic dogma because I was exploring my own emotional feelings. In the seventies it was very fashionable to read authors like Hermann Hesse and that gave me a terrific sense of being able to come to terms with why I was enjoying life and going to parties and being very flamboyant. For a while I was reading what I could about Buddhism, Hinduism, Taoism and other philosophies and I felt really good. Then, when I experienced illness and my mother died, I couldn't find any comfort in eastern philosophy so I turned back to the Christian religion. I made my pledge to God that if he pulled me through this, then I would dedicate my time to completing the Psalms as a sort of prayer.

In working through the Psalms have you found recurring themes that have given you an insight into yourself and your beliefs?

Yes, I think one of the main recurring themes is corruption, decadence and deceit. I am drawn to that for some reason, maybe because I used to think I was corrupt and I felt terrible about it, even though I see it as something very fundamental to human beings.

And the Psalms offer forgiveness?

The Psalms strike a chord of forgiveness and show us how hopeless we are without that ultimate love.

Another recurring theme is the trial.

I think we are under trial or being tested all the time. In fact I am so riddled with doubt and mistrust and suspicion that it feels like a sort of trial, as if He's testing me, so I am drawn to that type of imagery.

Is there a theological base to your investigations of the Psalms?

Not really, because from my knowledge of theologians in general and the parish priests in particular, they seem to look at the Psalms in a very literal way where I try to look beyond all that. So when I use certain symbols they think 'Oh, why is that there?', and when I point out the reason to them it makes sense, but it isn't a literal interpretation.

Can you describe how you find those images in the text as you read through each Psalm?

Well I read the Psalm to get a general feeling or mood. At times I find it difficult to get a vision, because they are visions, I'm not doing illustrations of the Psalms, so I put it away if nothing comes into my head because I find it very tormenting. Then I'll go back and maybe just one word in a verse will spark an image or a concept which I begin wrestling with on the canvas.

If you look at the way people are dressed and the objects that are in the rooms in your paintings, they are not of the present, instead they seem to inhabit the space and time of your childhood. Do you consciously situate the narratives in your past?

Through the eyes of a child, the men and women and my small village were a timeless people and their costume had a sort of volume and shape which grew out of an earthy simplicity. That's what struck in my mind from the time when I was able to recognise people until the time I came to Australia and I think they really became the fixed models of my life.

Did the Catholic imagery from that time have the same impact on your life as the people from the village?

My images, I suppose you could call them my heroes, were the local saints and as a child I didn't have the knowledge to appreciate that the image in front of me represented a 15th century or a 20th century or even a 21st century person. Instead, it represented a state of being that the people of the village modelled themselves on. So that's why I don't go for the chrome chair or the television set and in a way I am pleased because that has given me less clutter in my mind so that I can focus on what is really important — the human soul. You know it really doesn't matter what clothes we wear, it's what we feel. For example when we look at paintings of Munch or Goya, what strikes us is not so much the ornaments but the ways in which the artist was able to express universal human passions. There is no age in that and there is no century because emotions don't have limited slots in fashion.

Are you interested in the long history of artists who have located Biblical stories in their own world?

Yes! We can start with Piero della Francesca and move on to Rembrandt, then to Blake and Samuel Palmer, Stanley Spencer, Arthur Boyd and myself. All of these painters have the need to find their bearings by using their own worlds, which is basically their family and friends.

When you locate your pictures in Calabria or Australia do you see them as being typically Australian, Italian or as arising from a migrant experience?

I think the main source is Italian/Calabrian, and in recent years there have been glimpses where I have used the Australian landscape, but my landscape, as you have seen around Kurrajong, is more European. It has been Europeanised you know, so really I am seeing the landscape of Australia through the eyes of a European.

So you are not interested in the wild bush, it's the cultivated landscape that attracts you?

That's right, my inspiration is the European landscape which has been transported to Australia. So in a way I am living in a world of my own, a very Italian world which goes back to the memories of my childhood when I was living in Borgia, Calabria.

People have made the comparison between your work and that of Stanley Spencer and Fernando Botero. How important have these artists been in developing your own programme as an artist?

My first knowledge of Stanley Spencer was back in 1971 when I went on a student tour to see the great works of art and I remember seeing the Stanley Spencers in the Tate Gallery, but I wasn't really conscious of his work or what he was saying. I was more drawn to the works of Turner, for colour and light, and Blake at that time and at that phase of my evolution as a painter.

Then when I had that very traumatic experience of illness and then the following year the death of my mother, I think I was looking for a link of some kind that I could compare my images to other painters and get encouragement from them. The only person I came back to was Stanley Spencer. He was the only painter who came close to my method of using everyday experiences, because he also used his family and showed people as they were with their big, fat, wobbly legs. He used them to bring out the whole crescendo of emotion he portrayed and I could see a lot of my own spirit in his work. So when people saw the first batch of pictures it was understandable that they said 'Yes, that reminds me of Stanley Spencer', but when I had the chance to point out the link between Spencer and Giotto and the Italian painters of the *quattrocento*, who also used patterns of form and made use of the patterns on drapery as a part of their whole visual expression, then they saw how I had arrived at my interest in his work and how it related to my ideas.

And Botero?

Well I never knew about Botero until the last couple of years when a friend of mine brought this article to me and said, 'Look at this painting, your work is very much like Botero'. I could see the comparison in the way Botero uses his family situations and also the way he uses a voluptuous treatment of the figure, but in a very stilted manner, almost naive. It's not naive — you can't call it naive — and yet it's got a richness through his bold design and his feeling for flesh. Also Botero is said to be drawn to the world of corruption and so people have written and said, 'Oh yes, we know that's the same bordello and family scene thing that Botero is doing'. But Botero is new to me and so I think, great!, here's another painter living today, in another part of the world, who is doing something which is very personal and I feel encouraged by that.

The other source that is common to all three of you is an interest in folk art. How important is the link to the folk art of Calabria in your painting?

I think it is very important because that was another strong element in my childhood. The *per gracia ricevuta* images are a strong personal statement between you and the creator. If you're sick or there is something you want, especially a favour, then you make a painting of what's been given when it is granted to you. I think that has had an effect on me because when I was about seven or eight I was very popular in my street in the village, particularly with the women, because I had a great passion for making little images of the famous saints that I'd seen being taken through the streets on the men's shoulders. In my mother's house I would erect little shrines, the full stage you know, and I would create in my childish fantasy the full display of the saint's life. I would go down to the local creek and get bowls of clay and come back and do my little sculptures of each Saint or the Madonna. It was as real to me as it was for the grown-ups when they carried the big statues through the streets. I would re-enact the ceremony and ask my family to participate as I walked down the street with this little image. To me it was the full thing. Then in 1978, when my father went back to Borgia for the first time after years of living in Australia, one of the first questions they asked him was 'How is the little boy who used to come around and parade those images and ask for holy pictures for his collection?'. All that happened, and it's become like a big stewing pot in my mind and now it's coming out.

How do you go about painting one of the Psalms?

How? Well first of all I read the Psalm and I start thinking about images. The images I'm always drawn to in my mind are natural, family situations because that's where I know I can respond and make my statement. So I use natural settings and then I search for poses in natural situations. I'd be looking at magazines and films and I might see people in the city and make a mental note of an interesting face. From that I take a lot of photographs of the people around me when they're playing cards or sitting at the table. If I really want to construct an image I'm often drawn to some film stills and there I would be searching for a certain gesture which I want to incorporate. Using all these sorts of images I create my own amalgam.

Once I feel I'm getting to some sort of compositional structure, then I make lots of little drawings, even little scribbles, and then I might do a couple of pen and wash drawings. Finally I take a large canvas and square it up, because for me that old trick is the best way I know. It allows me to compose my forms easily.

When I'm doing that I'm not really concerned about trying to relate to individual figures but instead I treat them as shapes or forms within the whole. The composition must have that natural flow if it is not to be too contrived or static. I want to create a certain chaos and then allow the mood I'm seeking to come out of this, so the shapes start to appear in a natural way. Like when you make a head or a hand bigger because you want to intensify the emotion.

I normally use a conte or a pastel to do the drawing because I find charcoal makes my colours and my turps all murky and dirty. Then I block-in with a brush and finally the actual painting begins.

To get the light I want I normally start at the centre of the canvas and once I have one of those figures, or whatever shape it might be, a glass or a bottle or something, completed, I know how the whole life of the canvas can be related. So I don't work all over the surface, I just get stuck into one section and go from there. That's how it works.

Are you conscious of using Renaissance techniques such as glazing and making a feature of chiaroscuro?

Glazing, yes. I really feel that glazing techniques make the most of the pigments and in particular I like the translucent effect I get from glazing.

You also learned the techniques of fresco at one stage. Is that another example of working with traditional mediums?

Well, thinking back now to the little shrines you find on every corner in Calabria dedicated to some Saint or other, they were done in fresco. They were just a little column and a roof and the image of the Saint erected on the road as protection against the evil eye and to give a good harvest. I can remember as a child being taken by mother to our country farm and we would come across these various shrines. They had an impact on me, they really did, so I guess I was drawn to this continuing tradition of fresco painting in Italian art from Pompei to the present.

Also with fresco, if it's done properly, you get this beautiful luminosity. It just glows and you can apply the paint with a transparent, almost translucent, glaze. When it's done by the great guys like Giotto and those people, it's a wonderful, wonderful medium.

How important is Catholicism in your life?

Well for Italians it's not like it is for Irish Catholics or Methodists, who are in damnation from the beginning so that the poor individual is very oppressed. I don't feel like that. I can have a sexual experience with a woman, or go into a scene where there might be people in a hotel drinking or swearing or being rather obscene, and I don't walk away. I look and try to observe and understand or try to say, well this is another aspect of human beings, another texture or colour which I'm able to witness or participate in. Then by having that experience I know what it is like so that when I go after an image I want to portray in one of my paintings I'm better equipped to express that mood.

You see some Italians and Calabrians can very comfortably blaspheme the Virgin Mary or a Saint or the Holy Ghost or Christ because they have had a personal trauma over their children or themselves or because they are sick or in despair and turn towards God with anger, but the next day they will go to confession and take the bread and say their Hail Mary and they communicate with God and the Virgin Mary and they're fine. Life is warm and loving. You see we are all these things, we are angry, we feel pain, we feel jealousy, we hope to achieve better things. Of course we have all these elements in our character and you just can't put them aside because you are a Protestant or a Roman Catholic. They are part of one big woven image and each one is as important as the other. I'm very pleased that I have had this background. I was born in 1946 and the fifties were the beginning of television and I missed all that. Had I been born in a society like Australia or a modern industrial city like Milan, I wouldn't have had such a privileged existence. Borgia gave me time for my mind to develop, just like Garcia Lorca. He had time to develop and make his own world.

Your reference to Lorca brings up the question of literary sources in your work. Are there sources you constantly return to?

Well there's the Bible, I like Blake and Dante; Dante very much. Then I enjoy reading people like Robert Frost for example and some of T.S. Eliot and Dylan Thomas. I have used a few of Cavafi's poems for images, such as *Waiting for the Barbarians*, which is a great poem in which the male figure is idolised. If you read Cavafi you find that he too had a journey to fulfil. He went out into the street of Alexandria and looked for his image in the face of young men, while I look at my own family and friends to get the solace, the unified fulfillment, I seek. You see I think that by painting the Psalms I will get closer to some understanding of what God and life are all about. It's a form of meditation you know.

Are there other aspects of Italian popular culture that you use in your work?

Well I'm using Italian playing cards at the moment because I like the images and because I think it links me with my father and family, particularly my father. Thinking about his lifestyle and how he had to struggle has given me a personal language which I can use when referring to him. The cards all have eighteenth century men on horses, cavaliers or men with clubs and swords printed on them and they're very rich and very strong, particularly the suit of Spades.

And you associate these with men consorting together and doing deals?

Yes, both. The cards have a real link with the men. They are drawn together in this very male world which is the dominant scene in Italian society. The women are really the backbone of the family but the men are the ones that deal the cards. I see Italian cards and I see the Calabrian man. Everything he stands for is represented in a couple of cards, it's distilled into those images.

The image I use most of all is the man on the horse about to charge, the king and the sword. The man on the horse symbolises the journey through life, the king because we are all kings of our own lives, no matter what state our realm is in, and the sword is a symbol of cutting through whatever is mucking you around. It's also a very phallic, masculine image, domineering and brutal, so that's why I use it as well.

And the men are always seen in opposition to the women?

Yes, I think so. The men and the women are very much a unit on their own, but the women are very supportive. The woman is the mother figure, she is not looked upon as a threat or as a rival, as women often are in this society. The woman is seen by the Italian male as a loving, motherly figure, a person to love and look after and of course the mother of your kids.

Are there particular events in the religious year that have had an impact on your work?

In the cemetery of Borgia there is a chapel which has the most wonderful fresco of the angels descending into hell and taking souls up to heaven. That had a lasting impression on me. I can see it in my mind right now, like looking into a crystal ball and seeing all those wonderfully coloured chalky surfaces. Then at Easter they used to take the statue of the Virgin dressed in mourning and parade her on their shoulders through the streets. The whole thing was a drama, held at the break of day. People would be beating percussive instruments and drums and the children all followed along behind. Once or twice I participated by swinging the rattlers that accompanied our search for Jesus. It was very haunting, seeking after Christ along with the Virgin Mary. I think there is a link with the way the monks of Tibet play their bells and rattlers and horns and percussive instruments to arouse spirits from the depths of nature, the bowels of the earth. It creates an awesome awareness that something is happening or about to happen.

This seems to explain the incredible theatricality in your pictures and the sense of shared experience with the person you are representing. As you say, it's not just the Virgin Mary seeking Christ, you are seeking along with her.

Yes, most definitely we were seeking with her. We became a part of her search, we were an extension of her and it was very moving. Many women would cry when the image of the Virgin passed by because she represented the search of all mothers and all lovers for the things they love so dearly and for the pain they feel when the thing they have loved is sacrificed. That had a very emotional impact on the people, which is why it's such great theatre, such great drama.

Are your paintings trying to do the same thing?

I guess so. What I am trying to express is the constant search for fulfillment, like the quest of the Virgin Mary searching for Christ. There is a good sermon by Archbishop Fulton Sheen about the resurrection. Christ appeared to the apostles at the Sea of Galilee in the early morning mist and when Peter saw that it was Christ he didn't bother getting dressed, he just swam toward him and got halfway before he remembered that he had betrayed him three times. Later they lit a fire on the edge of the sea and Christ once again tested his love by asking Peter three times, saying 'Do you love me with a divine, totally committed, sacrificial love'. Each time Peter would say, 'Yes I love you in a human, natural, friendly kind of way'. But the third time the Lord said, 'Do you love me with a human, friendly, natural kind of love', and Peter was sad because the Lord seemed to doubt the other. But the Lord reached down and took the little love he had to offer and asked Peter to feed his lambs and feed his sheep. It was then that Peter realised that Christ takes a piece of our heart in the beginning of time and our heart's not complete without him, which is why we seek after that complete harmony, which is God.

And the people who look at your pictures, are you asking them to join your search?

Yes, to join my search and I want to arouse within them the feeling that this is not just a picture but much more than that. It's a statement of faith.

Sound pervades all the pictures. Why do your characters play trumpets, saxophones and drums?

You see in Borgia the church was both the theatre and the concert hall because on feast days or Saint's days they would have a brass band with percussive instruments and trumpets and it was wonderful.

Does your interest in the theatricality of the church explain your interest in the highly dramatic nature of Italian film-makers like Fellini and Pasolini?

Sure. I can link into them because Fellini, Pasolini, Visconti, all those Italian guys, seem to have had the same kind of childhood based on the Church and street theatre. The circus and the carousel came to town during religious festivals so I know that they were drawing on their childhood too, particularly Fellini. We are on the same wavelength and that's great.

Are you conscious of using a cinematic narrative technique? In some pictures the different episodes in the story happen within the picture and at other times it is almost as if you have set the scene before anything has happened so I'm interested in the way you develop strategies to tell your stories.

Well in *Psalm 17* I needed a complete cycle to tell the story. It was about an experience of deceit and betrayal that happened to me at the age of about three when a promise was broken and I used my memories to create a mood of anxiety and mistrust. It also links up with the Church and the brass band and the circus. The big circus fair which was held to celebrate the feast of the patron Saint of Borgia. I used all three events to tell this epic poem, or epic prayer. It was a prayer seen through a glass that has coloured my whole vision.

Then you became interested in the busker you saw in Florence and they took on a more theatrical presence, more like a stage set. Is that another strategy you have consciously employed?

Yes, I think so. Coming across the young busker in Florence opened a new vision of the stage as a vehicle to express these feelings and it also took me back to the time in Borgia when I saw circus people and gypsies. There is a link here with my childhood that enabled me to take inspiration from the modern day busker who set up a drama based on the anticipation of betrayal. Buskers and circus people are different from us, they make us aware of our own emotions and our own folly. At the same time I'm drawn to them because I see them as an image of disguised feelings. The scene behind the mask, like the sad clown who must go on and keep playing his role behind a painted smile. At the same time you must be wary because they might play a trick on you and mislead you. The busker in Florence was a young man in his early twenties who had the most basic props; a small trapeze, a cage and a old billy goat with a pom-pom on his head, a cat and a flaming hoop. I took lots of photographs of this bloke in action making his plain little tabby cat do these tricks and jump through the flaming hoop. It was painful to watch and I realised how I could use these images in my depiction of the Psalms to show how we exploit life and exploit each other.

When you returned to Australia you started a series of pictures using the busker in which you emphasised the stage set and used more intense, bright colour.

Just after I took those photographs I received a phone call from a member of my family to say that my father was dying and could I come back straight away. So I had to shorten my trip and come back to Australia to spend his last five weeks with him. I went to see him every day and because I knew he was dying it was really painful. I felt a lot of anger and a lot of frustration. The only way I was able to overcome my grief was to turn to my painting, and the image that came to me was the young busker putting his animals through those painful trials. The colours had to be as bright and intense as possible to express the sheer pain and anger I was experiencing.

This raises one of the most important questions. Are these religious paintings?

I think they are in a sense because I am using people, as I see them, to communicate to God an inner yearning within me. So I guess they are. Yes, they are! Even if the scene is a bordello it's a way for me to say that I am wrestling with my inner spirit, with my soul and my own torments. By trying to make these images of the

Psalms I am trying to get some sort of order out of my own emotional conflict. Yes, they are religious, but not in the sense of the Church, No!

And yet one of the Psalms *is hanging in a church?*

Yes, *Psalm 13*, is in St Kevin's Church in the Sydney suburb of Dee Why. It is really a gathering of people of all age groups, both men and women, who are trying to communicate with God so I presented that painting to the Church in memory of my mother. By seeing someone just like themselves, overweight and with all their varicose veins, the whole bloody lot, instead of some stylised image, I feel it has probably given the followers that go to that church an image they can relate to.

Are they moralising paintings?

No, they're not. I am not a moralist, I'm too busy struggling to keep myself in check, so how can I be a moralist? Far from it.

NOTES ON THE PAINTINGS
All measurements in centimetres, height before width.

Psalm 1
Oil on canvas, 1976,
101.6 x 127.1 cm.
Collection of Dr & Mrs J Murray, Sydney

Exhibited: Macquarie Galleries, 40 King Street, Sydney, 4–16 August 1976. The artist
also showed two smaller studies for this painting

Reviewed: Nancy Borlase, *Sydney Morning Herald*, 12 August 1976

The subject matter is very similar to another painting from the same period called *Sporaxis* (Oil on canvas, 1976, 71 x 91 cm.) in which a lush garden is separated from the viewer by a wire mesh fence. Zofrea emulates the Italian fifteenth century artists in this image of the gardener relocated in a space in which every element is precisely outlined and located in relation to the whole. There is no soft focus, just the intense stare of the believer. It is a device employed by the English painter Stanley Spencer whose re-siting of Biblical stories in his local village of Cookham served as a model for several of Zofrea's narratives based on the Psalms.

Psalm 2
Oil on canvas, 1976,
127.1 x 152.5 cm.
Private Collection, Perth

Exhibited: Macquarie Galleries, 40 King Street, Sydney, 4–16 August 1976

Illustrated: *Art & Australia*, Volume 14, Nos: 3 & 4, Summer–Autumn, 1977 Exhibition
Commentary

One of the most complex and successful paintings of the early Psalms, this powerful work introduces many potent images such as the king blinded by the symbol of his authority and the strong internal light which throws us into the middle of the drama.

Psalm 3

Oil on canvas, 1976,

122 x 152.5 cm.

Collection of Dr & Mrs R Hampshire, Sydney

Exhibited: Macquarie Galleries, 40 King Street, Sydney, 4–16 August 1976

Illustrated: *Salvatore Zofrea*, Stephanie Claire and Anna Waldmann, Hale & Iremonger, Sydney, p. 96

Australian Collectors Quarterly, May, June, July 1989

The large Resurrection paintings of Stanley Spencer, such as *The Resurrection: The Hill of Zion* of 1946, depict a similar mix of large figures locked together amongst a field of flowers in a jig-saw pattern. Spencer even went so far as to suggest these figures were 'shapes expressing the Resurrection ... they are not the shape of a human being, any more than the shape of a human being is the shape of the clay it was made from'[1]. Zofrea's figures have something of the same shell-like quality, though he is quick to point out that his interest in Spencer grew out of their shared respect for the work of Giotto and the early Renaissance painters Piero della Francesca and Botticelli.

1. *Stanley Spencer RA*, Royal Academy of Arts, Weidenfeld and Nicolson, London, 1980. p. 197.

Psalm 4
Oil on canvas, 1976,
122 x 152.5 cm.
Private Collection, Sydney

Exhibited: Macquarie Galleries, 40 King Street, Sydney, 4–16 August 1976

Illustrated: *The Weekend Australian*, 7–8 October 1988, *Salvatore Zofrea*, p. 97

The narrative component of the story is presented in a form which echoes the stylistic treatment found in Mannerist religious paintings. The change of scale of the figures and the division of the canvas into three sectors, showing the young girls, the three prostitutes and the male client, indicates that the artist was attracted to the idea of an altarpiece as the vehicle for this moral tale. The added piquancy of telling a bawdy tale in the guise of a religious painting and of linking the Biblical message to the format of the painting add to the intensity of the image.

Psalm 5
Oil on canvas, 1976,
61 x 76.2 cm.
Collection of the Cafe du Paris, Melbourne

Exhibited: Macquarie Galleries, 40 King Street Sydney, 4–16 August 1976

Illustrated: 'You can go out & draw', Sally McInerney the *Sydney Morning Herald*, 5 August 1976

'Mostre d'arte: 15 ma personale di Salvatore Zofrea', *Globo*, 8 August 1976

In this painting, Zofrea introduces an analysis of the ways in which individuals perceive the world, as a counter-balance to his more usual depiction of the world as a series of physically present objects. The everyday world of material objects is dissolved in the blurriness of 'real' visual experience.

As the material density of objects in the world is such a crucial element in his depiction of the continuing presence of the spiritual in our lives, this formal device is significant in subverting that reading. Instead the central figure is intensely 'there', while her environment is conditional on our gaze.

Not surprisingly Zofrea did not continue with this device because it undermined his premise that the world is a physical manifestation of God's law.

Psalm 6

Oil on canvas, 1976,

50.8 x 61 cm.

Private collection, North Queensland

Illustrated: Cover of the Sydney catalogue (in black and white)

Study for Psalm 6

Watercolour, 1976,

30 x 45.7 cm.

Collection of Treania Smith, Sydney

Exhibited: Macquarie Galleries, 40 King Street, Sydney, 4–16 August 1976

Macquarie Galleries, 35 Murray Crescent, Manuka, Canberra, 18 August–4 September 1977

Illustrated: Cover of the Sydney catalogue (in black and white)

The watercolour sketch is in the collection of Treania Smith who was joint owner of the Macquarie Galleries when these works were first shown.

Psalm 7

Oil on canvas, 1976,

101.6 x 132.2 cm.

Mary Turner Collection, Orange New South Wales Regional Gallery

Exhibited: Macquarie Galleries, Sydney, 4–16 August, 1976. Cat. No. 9

Illustrated: *Salvatore Zofrea*, p. 112.

The Mary Turner Collection of the Orange Regional Gallery, the Orange City Council, 1982

Stanley Spencer used a similar break-up of space in his *The Resurrection with the Raising of Jairus's Daughter*, painted in 1947, to indicate the unsuspected presence of the metaphysical in the most commonplace surroundings. The elevated vantage point used in this picture releases viewers from the everyday considerations of gravity, making it much easier to believe in the extraordinary visitation. The ruptured perspective of the house within the ordered garden might have looked rather awkward if it weren't for the artist's physical realignment of his audience.

In her excellent article on the artist's work in *Salvatore Zofrea*, Anna Waldmann describes this painting as 'full of anguish' and suggests that it illustrates the lines 'Arise, O Lord, in thine rage ... and awake for me to the judgement that thou hast commanded'. This interpretation is at variance with mine. The expression on the sick man's face and the sense of calm that pervades the picture does not imply anguish and Zofrea's own suggestion that he illustrated the first verse seems to confirm this reading.

Psalm 8 — Noah's Ark

Oil on canvas, 1976,
198 x 274 cm.
Collection of the Bar Association of New South Wales, Sydney

Exhibited: Although not exhibited at Macquarie Galleries exhibition in Sydney, 4–16 August 1976, three oil studies on board, one in watercolour and another etching *Study for Psalm 8*, were included.

Illustrated: *Salvatore Zofrea*, p. 52

The artist's mother died in 1976 and the artist Henry Justelius, who was a mentor to the young Zofrea, died in the same year. Their deaths were a severe blow at a time when he was very ill himself.

The source for much of the imagery came from the artist's sketches of people at Clontarf Beach near the family home at Seaforth, Sydney. The beach was an escape from the routines of suburban life and the artist walked there several afternoons a week with painter Lillian Sutherland. It provided a model for a calmer environment, apart from everyday concerns. Many of the figures in this painting were drawn from people sitting at the beach, although the seated male bather on the extreme left is so reminiscent of Seurat's *Baignade a Asnieres* that it may have arisen through an unconscious infiltration. During months of convalescence in 1975 Zofrea went to Taronga Park Zoo every other day and drew the animals. These pen and wash studies were shown at Macquarie Galleries in November under the title of 'Zofrea's Zoo'. A sellout exhibition it also provided the research for the birds and animals in this painting.

The artist's interest in Rembrandt and the *quattrocento* Italian masters was further support for this method of contemporising Biblical stories and within the Australian context the location of Noah's selection of the animals for inclusion on the ark at Clontarf Beach echoes Arthur Boyd's siting of Old Testament stories in Melbourne.

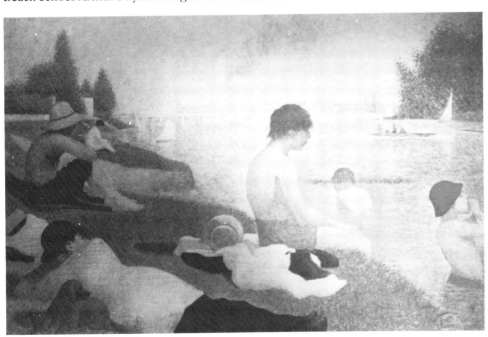

Psalm 9
Oil on canvas, 1976,
71.2 x 96.5 cm.
Private Collection, Sydney

Exhibited: Macquarie Galleries, 40 King Street, Sydney, 4–17 August 1976

Macquarie Galleries, 35 Murray Crescent, Manuka, Canberra, 18 August–
4 September 1977

The elements of this painting were developed from the artist's imagination and his store of
visual memories. During his recuperation the previous year he visited the Zoo regularly to
draw the animals and birds, exhibiting them in November of that year. This experience
and the environment of his parents' home, where he was living, were the source for the
imagery in this work.

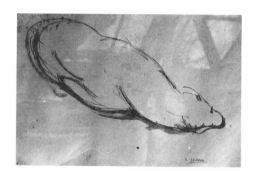

Psalm 10
Oil on canvas, 1976,
61 x 45.7 cm.
Collection of Mr and Mrs G Jones

Symbolism plays a crucial role in the artist's construction of his pictures and in this study of his mother eating her meal by an open window, the light that pours into the room is adopted as a traditional symbol for the presence of Christ. Similarly the bread represents Holy Communion and the choice of evening is significant because of the association with forbearance and the passing of time. These literary clues are very important in the artist's lexicon of narrative devices and must be understood if the paintings are to be decoded. His exploration of traditional symbolism and his invention of a personal symbology is indicative of his lively yet reflective attitude to the tradition of painting. He is quite willing to borrow from religious themes or earlier iconography when it fits his own programme and to juxtapose these against imagery from his own experience. In this new context it assumes a more universal significance and we are encouraged to read it as charged with meaning.

Psalm 11
Oil on canvas, 1976,
71 x 91.5 cm.
Collection of Tracy Mulligan, Sydney

Exhibited: Macquarie Galleries, 35 Murray Crescent, Manuka, Canberra, 18 August–
              4 September 1977

There is always a tension between the objective depiction of the world as it presents itself
to the eye and the artist's inner reality. In this painting Zofrea employs a detached objective treatment of the scene from his bedroom window in the family home at Seaforth, but
injects a very specific narrative in the form of the ladybird. This is made palpably real by his
matter-of-fact description of the material world of lace curtain, wood, walls and garden.
They are rendered with such naive clarity that we cannot avoid accepting them as containing deeper meaning. They become material symbols which he has conjured up out of an
anonymous material world.

Psalm 12 — Song of Songs (Song of Solomon)
Oil on canvas, 1976,
152.5 x 183 cm.
Collection of James Fairfax, Bowral

Exhibited: Macquarie Galleries, 40 King Street, Sydney, 4–16 August 1976. Two watercolour studies for this work were also shown in the same exhibition.

Illustrated: Salvatore Zofrea, p. 51

        'Salvatore Zofrea', Anna Waldmann, *Art & Australia*, Vol 19, No. 3, Autumn 1982

The imagery is derived from Zofrea's research into Italian *quattrocento* painting, his interest in Stanley Spencer's painting, his collection of photographs gathered from magazines and his own drawings. The arching yellow leaves at the top of the composition are borrowed from an illustration on the cover of a recording of Virgil Thompson and Gertrude Stein's opera, 'Four Saints in Three Acts'.

Psalm 13 — Opening of the Fifth Seal
Oil on canvas, 1976,
76 x 51 cm. 91 x 61 cm. 76 x 51 cm. (triptych)
Collection of St Kevin's Catholic Church, Dee Why, Sydney (donated by the artist)

Exhibited: Macquarie Galleries, 40 King Street, Sydney, 4–16 August 1976. Four watercolour studies for this painting were also shown in the same exhibition.

Illustrated: *Salvatore Zofrea*, pp 98–99.

        'Salvatore Zofrea', Anna Waldmann, *Art & Australia*, Vol 19, No. 3, Autumn 1982

The triptych form was used quite consciously because of its religious overtones so it was appropriate that it found its final home in a church. The artist donated it to the Dee Why church in memory of his mother.

       The figures are drawn from family members and friends, some of whom posed for the artist while others were 'just around'. At the bottom of the composition the open book represents the 'book of life' in which the record of each life is kept. All of the new arrivals will be assessed on the basis of this volume and assigned their rightful place in heaven.

Psalm 14 — Que Dice Donna Dice Donna
Oil on canvas, 1978,
184 x 198 cm.
Private Collection, Sydney

Exhibited: Sulman Prize, Art Gallery of New South Wales 1978

'Recent works by Figurative Painters', Macquarie Galleries, 40 King Street, Sydney, 26 April–15 May 1978

Illustrated: *Salvatore Zofrea* (front cover)

'A Religious Surrealist', Paul White, *Follow Me*, December 1983

'Salvatore Zofrea', *The Australian*, 26 September 1983

There are many sources for individual elements within Zofrea's paintings. The men in the composition and the girl were transcribed from a black and white still from an Italian movie he had found in a magazine. Its title was also borrowed from the film by Tonino Cervi, *Que Dice Donna Dice Donna*. The carpet is from his home, the oriental wall decorations from a screen. Each element is then wrenched from its previous context and welded into the new 'reality' constructed by the artist. This process is sometimes done very smoothly with no seam allowed to show through, however, a certain collaged quality is evident in this painting. It is his way of emphasising the awkwardness of the situation and the artifice of the brothel.

Psalm 15 — Te Deum
Oil on canvas, 1984,
229 x 604 cm. (triptych)
Private Collection, Sydney

Exhibited: Sulman Prize, Art Gallery of New South Wales, 1984

Illustrated: Macquarie Galleries postcard

The landscape around Kurrajong in the Blue Mountains outside Sydney, where the artist lives, is the setting for this painting and the individuals in heaven are all drawn from his family and friends. They are memory portraits more than observational studies, recording their personalities and their importance to the artist.

The flowers, on the other hand, are painted from examples in the artist's garden. Like his father, Zofrea is also a gardener — a man rooted in the earth — but instead of planting only things that can be eaten, he prefers to grow flowers.

Psalm 16

Oil on canvas, 1988,
195 x 300 cm.
Private Collection, Sydney

Exhibited: Sulman Prize, Art Gallery of New South Wales, 1988

The role of photographs and cinema stills as source material in Zofrea's work did cause a minor uproar when several readers of *The Bulletin* responded to an article by Geoffrey Dutton, published in 1984, which included a photograph of the painting *Girls at Clontarf*. They pointed out that the artist had used photographs by Richard Hamilton as source material and placed them into a new context. While the arguments on both sides were interesting Zofrea explained: 'I did use his images but then I transformed them into my environment ... They are used in a different setting and that gives the painting a different meaning.'[1]

In this painting the source for the figure of the young boy is a still from a movie called *The Mirror* reproduced in *Film and Filming*. Cinema has made a significant impact on Zofrea. The dramatic possibilities of cinema direction and the ambience and Baroque lighting found in film, (in particular those of Italian directors like Fellini, Pasolini and Visconti) are a major influence on the artist's sense of narrative and the use of stills from these films is another device he employs in his quest to charge his pictures with the drama of the movies.

1.   Lenore Nicklin, 'Inspiration or Imitation — That's the Question', *The Bulletin*, 10 April 1984, pp 68–69.

Psalm 17

Oil on canvas, 1988,

195 x 300 cm.

Private Collection, Sydney

Exhibited: Sulman Prize, Art Gallery of New South Wales, 1988

This painting is based on a childhood memory. However, the most important elements are those that the artist has invented. The succinct images of adult sexuality, the claustrophobic space (reminiscent of the German painter Max Beckmann) the association with the deceit Christ suffered and the hope of redemption described in the painting on the wall, are all ways in which the artist has injected this painting with his own anguish.

Some of the figures were developed from friends who posed for the artist, others were translated from photographs and the rest were re-invented from the artist's memories.

Psalm 18 — La Notte Di Rosignano
Oil on canvas, 1987,
180 x 240 cm.
Collection of George Pattersons, Sydney

Exhibited: Macquarie Galleries, 204 Clarence Street, Sydney, 8–24 December 1987

Illustrated: *First Australian Contemporary Art Fair*, Catalogue, Melbourne, 1988

Salvatore Zofrea, Paintings, Catalogue, Macquarie Galleries, 1988

The figures spending the night at the Rosignano Cafe are, according to the artist, ' a mixture of Fellini and Zofrea'. The Italian film director's famous film *La Dolce Vita* sets the tone for this painting and some of the figures are translated from film stills, however, the two central characters are once again family and friends. The girl at the table is his niece Teresa Zofrea and the boy with the candle is Ben Dowling. These elements have been fused together in an ambience borrowed from films like, Rainer Werner Fassbinder's film of Jean Genet's novel, *Querelle*. The small village of Rosignano and its neighbour Quercianella are seaside resorts in Tuscany, opposite the Isle of Elba, which the artist visited while studying fresco techniques with Leonetto Tintori on a Churchill Fellowship in 1986. The Christian symbolism of the open book and the single, lit candle recurs frequently in his Psalms while the image of the cat drinking and the drained bottles and glasses are just as readable as symbols of wasted opportunities.

Psalm 19 — La Grande Promessa
Oil on canvas, 1987,
180 x 270 cm.
Collection of the Darling Harbour Authority, Sydney

Exhibited: Macquarie Galleries, 204 Clarence Street, Sydney, 8–24 December 1987

This is the first of a series of *Psalms* based on photographs of a young busker and his troupe of performing animals which the artist took in Florence in 1987. The bulk of the imagery is derived from these photographs, although the bird cage is in the possession of the artist and the figure of the boy sitting on the drum is a portrait of Ben Dowling. The theatrical devices of artificial stage sets and frontal presentation used in this series replace the more cinematic lighting and narrative developed in the previous nocturnal images.

References: See the interview included in this volume.

Psalm 20 — The Visitors
Oil on canvas, 1987,
180 x 270 cm.
Collection of A C Arnold & Associates, Melbourne

Exhibited: Macquarie Galleries, 204 Clarence Street, Sydney, 8–24 December 1987

First Australian Contemporary Art Fair, Exhibition Hall, Melbourne, 23–31 July 1988

Illustrated: 'The Secret of Fresh Frescos', Sally Blakeney, *The Weekend Australian*, 5–6 December 1987

Salvatore Zofrea, Paintings, Catalogue, Macquarie Galleries, 1988

This painting is the second based on the 1987 photographs of the Florentine busker, with the addition of the young prostitute from *Psalm 14 — Que Dice Donna Dice Donna*, a neighbour from Kurrajong (the second figure from the right) and a fat woman seen on trips through the town of Richmond, New South Wales. Other figures are translated from photographs and film stills to expand the theme of the *Psalm* into a more universal statement of redemption.

References: See the interview reproduced in this volume.

Psalm 21 — Il Padrone
Oil on canvas, 1987,
150 x 165 cm.
Private Collection, Adelaide

Exhibited: Macquarie Galleries, 204 Clarence Street, Sydney, 8–24 December 1987

Once again the basic imagery of the painting is derived from photographs of the young busker in Florence, with the addition of the king from *Psalm 2* and a young woman combing her hair, which the artist painted from a model.

References: See the interview reproduced in this volume.

Psalm 22
Oil on canvas, 1982,
198 x 243 cm.
Private Collection, Sydney

Exhibited: Macquarie Galleries, 204 Clarence Street, Sydney, 30 November–
18 December 1982

Illustrated: *Salvatore Zofrea*, p. 79

The two men at the bottom right of the painting shaking hands over a deal are drawn from a still from the film *The War Lord* while the young man is painted from a model. As with many paintings in this series, it is a mixture of imagery from photographs, the artist's family and friends, his own paintings from a model, and other art which he has translated and then re-combined.

The image of the girl is developed from a traditional pose similar to that used by the French-Polish artist Balthus in several paintings and the Christ Crucified is copied from a painting on the cover of a recording of Bach's *St Matthew Passion*. This painting by an unknown Flemish master is one of the few images in history of an angry Christ giving vent to his frustration in the face of his persecutors.

Psalm 23

Oil on canvas, 1978,

127 x 152 cm.

Collection of the World Bishops' Boardroom Hall, Vatican Museum, Rome

Illustrated: *Quadrant*, March 1982 (Frontispiece)

A Painting that 'comes from Australia' for the Pope 'who comes from afar'. *La Fiamma* 24 March 1978

'Roman dream comes true for Painter', *The Australian*, 21 June 1979

'From Paddy's Market to the Vatican', *Women's World*, 17 October 1979

The major source for this image is a photograph of a Mormon baptism in the book *In this Proud Land — America 1935–43 as seen in the FSA Photographs*,[1] with a change of location to the Hawkesbury river and the inclusion of members of his family and friends on the bank observing the event.

1.   Roy Emerson Stryker and Nancy Wood, New York Graphic Society, Boston Massachusetts, 1973.

References: A Painting that 'comes from Australia' for the Pope 'who comes from afar'. *La Fiamma*, 24 March 1978

Psalm 24 — In Heaven

Oil on canvas, 1982,

243 x 395 cm. (diptych)

Gift of Eileen Chanin and Adrian Morris 1983, Collection of the Art Gallery of New South Wales

Exhibited: Macquarie Galleries, 204 Clarence Street, Sydney, 30 November– 18 December 1982

Sulman Prize, Art Gallery of New South Wales, 1982 (Winner)

Illustrated: *Salvatore Zofrea*, p. 62–63

Although painted four years later than the previous *Psalm* this painting is also sited along the Hawkesbury River around Kurrajong, where the artist lives. Many of the characters are drawn from his family and friends with his mother and grandfather taking a central role in the right hand panel of the painting.

Psalm 25

Oil on canvas, 1982,

183 x 198 cm.

Collection of Mr and Mrs M Page, Sydney

Exhibited: Macquarie Galleries, 204 Clarence Street, Sydney, 30 November–
              18 December 1982

Illustrated: *Salvatore Zofrea*, p. 66

This is an extremely complex painting which the artist pieced together from images he found in photographs, his domestic environment and from amongst his friends. The model is a friend and the young boy is Ben Dowling. The young girl is Loren, the daughter of a friend, who is also the subject of the next *Psalm*.

Playing cards are an increasingly important image in the paintings that follow, both as a pastime and as a source of imagery. In this work the men playing cards were photographed at Bondi Beach and the Italian playing cards on the floor are the same as those used by his father and friends. The upside down parrot appears in many of the paintings to indicate that all is not right. Similarly darkness and night scenes are generally interpreted as ominous in Zofrea's pictorial constructions. The moon that appears outside the window is echoed in the thin moon that hangs above Christ's head in the painting on the wall and can be read as a symbol of incompleteness.

Psalm 26 (Loren)

Oil on canvas, 1982,
153 x 168 cm.
Private Collection, Sydney

Exhibited: Macquarie Galleries, 204 Clarence Street, Sydney, 30 November–
18 December 1982

Illustrated: *Salvatore Zofrea*, p. 128

'A Religious Surrealist', Paul William-White, *Follow Me*, December 1983

Loren, the daughter of a friend, was eleven years old when she posed for this painting and *Psalm 25*. The landscape is drawn from around Kurrajong where the artist lives and works.

Psalm 27 — From St Paul's Letters to the Corinthians

Oil on canvas, 1977,
90 x 120 cm.
Private collection, Canberra

Photograph: Sally McInerney

Zofrea has often used photographs as source material for his paintings and *The Family of Man*, a collection of photographs selected by Edward Streichen and published by the Museum of Modern Art in New York in 1955, has been an important treasury of images. This painting is based on a photograph of Russian peasants by Robert Capa, reproduced on page 92 of that book. The central image of the figures has then been translated by the artist into the village of Borgia in Calabria where he was born.

Psalm 28

Oil on canvas, 1982,

153 x 168 cm.

Collection of the University of Sydney

Exhibited: Macquarie Galleries, 204 Clarence Street, Sydney, 30 November–18 December 1982

Illustrated: *Salvatore Zofrea*, p. 60

                 'Sales are the prizes at Uni exhibitions', Susanna Short, *Sydney Morning Herald*, 3 November 1983

The major source for this work is a photograph by David Hamilton which the artist found in a book. He then asked a friend to pose in a similar way and painted the final image of the girl. Many of the other figures are friends or family members painted from memory, photographs or from life. As well as the two icons of Mary on the wall the themes of the other religious paintings are Christ in Majesty, the Annunciation and, at the centre, the Pentecost.

Psalm 29 — Il Sogno

Oil on canvas, 1987,

150 x 165 cm.

Collection of the Artist

Exhibited: Macquarie Galleries, 204 Clarence Street, Sydney, 8–24 December 1987

The central figure is painted from a life model while the field in which she is lying is constructed from the artist's imagination and his knowledge of art history. This juxtaposition of two modes of representation creates the dynamic tension between everyday reality and the reality of the dream, indicated in the subtitle. By association it also encapsulates the artist's belief in peace after death and a final resurrection in heaven.

Psalm 30 — Rosa
Oil on canvas, 1987,
120 x 150 cm.
Courtesy of Macquarie Galleries, Sydney

Exhibited: Macquarie Galleries, 204 Clarence Street, Sydney, 8–24 December 1987

Vincent Art Gallery, Adelaide, August 1989

Recent Australian Art, Houston International Festival, Texas (Represented by Macquarie Galleries)

Rosa is based on an etching the artist made of two lovers he encountered at Clontarf in the mid-seventies (reproduced in *Salvatore Zofrea*, p. 92). Although many details are changed the dynamic presence of the man's thigh and foot pressing down on his girlfriend's leg remains the central image in this painting.

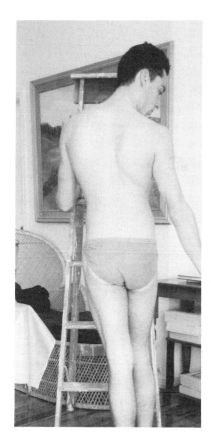

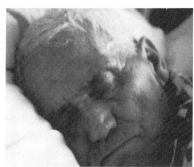

Psalm 31 — Death and Transfiguration

Oil on canvas, 1987,

300 x 195 cm.

Courtesy of Macquarie Galleries, Sydney

Exhibited: Macquarie Galleries, 204 Clarence Street, Sydney, 8–24 December 1987

Zofrea took photographs of the young busker in Florence before he left Italy to be at his father's side during his final illness. These photographs were the source for much of the imagery used in this series of six paintings. The image of his father was translated from one of his photographs taken during his father's illness.

Childhood is one of the major sources of imagery for the artist who plumbs his memory for those experiences that so enriched his early years in Calabria. The Easter parades with drums and rattles and the acknowledgment of death and respect for those that have died are traditions that were brought with the Italian community to Australia. Significant days such as *Il giorno di morte* (the day of the dead), when families spruce up gravestones and take time to commune with their loved-ones, are still important events in his calendar.

Psalm 32 — The Carousel

Oil on canvas, 1987,

225 x 195 cm.

Collection of Macquarie Galleries, Sydney

Exhibited: Macquarie Galleries, 204 Clarence Street, Sydney, 8–24 December 1987

Memories of the Uccello painting in the Uffizi were revived when the artist came across a carousel at a park in Sydney. The white horse reminded him of the painting and also of the Italian playing cards that his father and friends used so frequently. The juxtaposition of these three elements plays an increasingly important role in the *Psalms* that follow. The young man, in this and other paintings from this period is based on photographs taken in the streets in Florence. His strength of character and Renaissance demeanour were so compelling that Zofrea used his image in several paintings.

Psalm 33 — Il Circo del Mare
Oil on canvas, 1987,
195 x 225 cm.
Courtesy of Macquarie Galleries, Sydney

Exhibited: Macquarie Galleries, 204 Clarence Street, Sydney, 8–24 December 1987

As with *Psalm 31* the source for the imagery in this painting is a series of photographs the artist took of a busker and a young man in the street in Florence during a study tour in 1986. The saxophone held by the young man was chosen by the artist because of its phallic association (blowing his own horn) and its earthy sound. Also in *Verse 2* of the Psalm believers are exhorted to praise the Lord with musical instruments.

Psalm 34 — I Giorni Sono Contati
Oil on canvas, 1987,
225 x 195 cm.
Courtesy of Macquarie Galleries, Sydney

Exhibited: Macquarie Galleries, 204 Clarence Street, Sydney, 8–24 December 1987

Like his fellow countryman, Frederico Fellini, Salvatore Zofrea has been absorbed by the bizarre world of circuses, clowns and fairgrounds. Just as Fellini often uses the action of the fairground to comment on the life of his characters, so Zofrea employs clowns and the props of the circus as a metaphor for the trials and tribulations of our temporal existence. This is reflected in the sub-title, 'The Days are Counted'. The theatricality of the film world, and of Fellini's films in particular, has always attracted the artist and as well as borrowing ideas from stills he has often sought a similar ambience. One recurring image Fellini uses is the night scene lit by rows of lights, and Zofrea acknowledges him as the source for this image. As in the other pictures of this series, the photographs of the busker in Florence provide most of the imagery. The toucan was photographed in a pet shop at the same time, and the young man in based on photographs of Ben Dowling.

Psalm 35 — After Uccello
Oil on canvas, 1988,
198 x 300 cm.
Collection of Mr and Mrs M Page, Sydney

Exhibited: 'Painters Visions', Macquarie Galleries, 204 Clarence Street, Sydney, 29 May–17 June 1989

Sulman Prize, Art Gallery of New South Wales, 1988

Illustrated: 'Collectables', *Australian Business* 6 June 1990

Contemporary Australian Painting, ed. Eileen Chanin, Craftsman House, Sydney, 1990

Postcard by Macquarie Galleries

The Italian playing cards that Zofrea uses in many of his paintings of the Psalms were familiar to him through his childhood and in earlier scenes of card playing the men are playing with these cards. The artist also associates their imagery of mounted soldiers, swords and war plumes with his father, whose death in 1986 sparked-off the group of works exploring the imagery of the busker and Uccello's paintings. The source for this work is *The Battle of San Romano*, (Tempera on wood, 182 x 323 cm., 1456) in the collection of the Uffizi, Florence.

Psalm 36
Watercolour, 1988,
48 x 60 cm.
Private Collection, Sydney

The imagery of this painting is derived from two previous paintings in the series, *Psalms 16* and *25*, with the addition of the rug from the artist's home and the details of a room drawn from his past experiences.

Psalm 37 — After Uccello II

Oil on canvas, 1989,

178 x 306 cm.

Courtesy of Macquarie Galleries, Sydney

Exhibited: Sulman Prize, Art Gallery of New South Wales 1989

'Inside World', Macquarie Galleries, 204 Clarence Street, Sydney 13–31 March 1990

Illustrated: 'Inside World', Catalogue

Postcard by Macquarie Galleries

The Uccello *Rout of San Romano* in the National Gallery in London is the model for this painting and the Etruscan soldiers on the right of the painting are translated from photographs in *The Art of the Etruscans*, M. Pallottino, Thames & Hudson, London, 1955, pp. 240–243. As in the earlier paintings from his series, the cards in the foreground are based on the traditional Italian playing cards.

At this time the artist purchased the family home in Seaforth and made a second studio there. Although recovering from his illness, he worked diligently on this picture, producing a series of watercolour studies which he exhibited at the Macquarie Galleries in 1989.

Psalm 38

Oil on canvas, 1988,
120 x 180 cm.
Private Collection, Sydney

Zofrea visited Quercianella when he was in Italy on his Churchill Fellowship and the photographs he took there became the setting for both this *Psalm* and *Psalm 40*. Richard Diebenkorn's painting *Interior with Book* from 1959, reproduced in Gerald Nordland, *Richard Diebenkorn*, Rizzoli, New York, 1987, p. 105, was also a source for the blue colouration and the ambience of the room.

Psalm 39

Oil on canvas, 1978,
183 x 137 cm.
Private Collection, Sydney

Illustrated: 'Salvatore Zofrea', by Anna Waldmann, *Art & Australia*, Vol 19, No. 3, Autumn 1982

The photograph by Lee titled 'Visiting relatives' graves on All Saint's Day: New Roads, Louisiana' is reproduced in the book *In this Proud Land — America 1935–43 as seen in the FSA Photographs*.[1] It forms the core of this painting although the location was changed to the cemetery in French's Forest where the artist's mother is buried. See also *Psalm 23* which is also based on a photograph from this book.

1.   Roy Emerson Stryker and Nancy Wood, New York Graphic Society, Boston, Massachusetts, 1973.

Psalm 40 — Afternoon at Quercianella

Oil on canvas, 1987,

195 x 240 cm.

Private Collection

The artist's photographs taken at Quercianella on the Mediterranean coast of Tuscany, were the prime source for the setting of this painting. Into this environment he placed a portrait of Sally Dowling, also based on his own photographs.

Psalm 41
Oil on canvas, 1989,
150 x 165 cm.
Private Collection, Sydney

Much of the imagery used in this *Psalm* is derived from other paintings in this series. The ladder appears firstly in the group of paintings inspired by the busker in Florence and the musical instruments and the cage are often recurring images. Italian playing cards have also become an important motif symbolising fate, gambling and masculinity.

The dog is translated from photographs of the figures from Pompeii that were covered with ash and turned to stone when Mount Vesuvius erupted. The dog, caught in its last death throes, is one of the memorable images from that group of photographs.

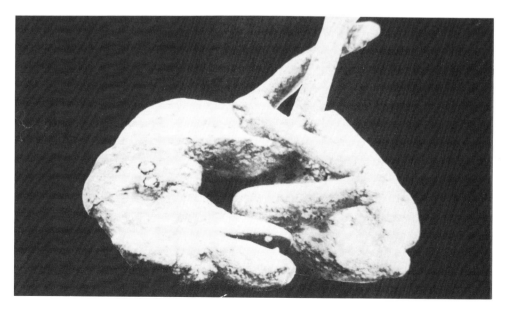

Psalm 42

Oil on canvas, 1989,

150 x 165 cm.

Private Collection, Sydney

The double-headed eagle is borrowed from the Italian playing cards where it is the equivalent of the Ace of Diamonds. Zofrea has used it in this context to signify the power of the female over the male and the problems that ensue for the man caught in the trap of his own desires.

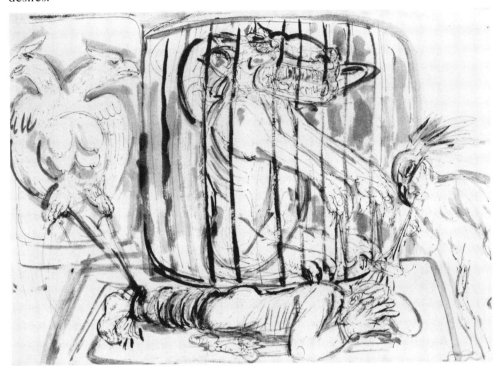

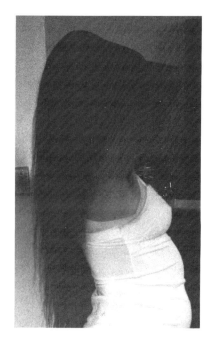

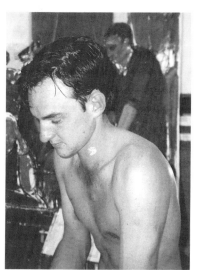

Psalm 43
Oil on canvas, 1989,
120 x 150 cm.
Private Collection, Sydney

The Italian playing cards are different in number and suits from other cards, so their use is significant for the artist in establishing his heritage and placing this activity at the heart of his family life. Although the works of the Colombian artist Fernando Botero have not greatly influenced Zofrea, the woman combing her hair does have an affinity with his work. She evolved from studies of a model, then, because he wanted to portray gluttony, he made the figure grotesque. Nevertheless, her bulky form does echo Botero's inflated belles. The two male figures are based on studies of Ben Dowling and a student who occasionally modelled for the artist.

Psalm 44 — After Uccello III
Oil on canvas, 1990,
195 x 300 cm.
Courtesy of Macquarie Galleries, Sydney

Exhibited: Archibald Prize, Art Gallery of New South Wales, 1990

Macquarie Galleries, 85 McLachlan Avenue, Rushcutters Bay, 12 February
–9 March 1991

This is the final painting based upon the three versions of Uccello's *Battle of San Romano*,
held in the collections of the Uffizi, the National Gallery in London and the Louvre. Each
picture introduces different imagery and ideas, even though the basic structures of
Uccello's originals are maintained. For this version, the artist had himself photographed
riding on a merry-go-round, wearing a replica of the turban worn by the central character in
the Uccello painting. He then transposed himself into the painting, converting it into a
personal document that confronts his self-image as an Italian artist and his sense of anger
and frustration after many years of illness.

Psalm 45
Oil on canvas, 1991,
107 x 122 cm.
Collection of the artist

The woman curled up in a foetal position being seduced by the centaur is developed from studies of a friend. The artist explains that the choice of the pose was important because it suggested that the woman had become the victim of her circumstances.

Psalm 46
Oil on canvas, 1990,
150 x 180 cm.
Courtesy of Macquarie Galleries, Sydney

The young man in this painting is based on photographs and studies of a young student whom the artist occasionally employs to model for him. Most of the artist's models are chosen from his family and friends because of the need to become very familiar with their physical features and also their characters. The faces which recur frequently throughout the series are his own family and that of his friend Stephanie Claire, whose two children Ben and Sally Dowling also appear in many paintings. This young student is an exception, though he also appears in *Psalm 43*.

Psalm 47

Oil on canvas, 1989,

120 x 180 cm.

Courtesy of Macquarie Galleries, Sydney

Exhibited: Mandorla Prize for Religious Art, New Norcia, Western Australia, 1989

Illustrated: 'Theft puts Australian art in good hands', *The West Australian*, 4 November,
               1989, p. 5

This picture was painted at the same time as *Psalm 37 — After Uccello II* using similar pictorial ideas. The donkey on the skateboard replicates the horse on its tiny set of wheels and the central character holding on to his horse in such an awkward way is based on an idea introduced in *Psalm 37*. The larger source for the painting is the village of Borgia. Although it is an ever-present force behind many of the pictures this is the only *Psalm* in which the village appears as a leading character.

Psalm 48

Oil on canvas, 1991,

122 x 107 cm.

Courtesy of Macquarie Galleries, Sydney

This painting was begun as a diptych. However, as it grew and evolved, the artist became discouraged with the format and concentrated on the first panel in which two men watch as the centaur seduces a woman. One figure represents temporal power, but as the artist explains 'His hand covers his face because he has witnessed that the heart can betray him and although he has authority, he knows he hasn't power over the heart and the pain it can cause.'[1]

1.   Letter from the artist, 11 March 1991.

Psalm 49

Oil on canvas, 1991,

125 x 180 cm.

Collection of the artist

Many of the pictorial devices used in this *Psalm* are derived from a series of photographs the artist took of the busker in Florence while he was undertaking a Churchill Fellowship research project in 1986 and the other figures are developed from photographs taken by the artist.

Psalm 50

Oil on canvas, 1991,

120 x 180 cm.

Courtesy of Macquarie Galleries, Sydney

Zofrea often mines previous paintings for imagery with the consequence that they form their own internal narratives within the larger story of the *Psalms*. The sequence of paintings that include the young couple in an intimate embrace shows a progressive deterioration in their projected future. The artist is suggesting that their first sexual encounter starts them on an inexorable decline into frustration and separation. Seen together these three depictions of the couple, drawn from different paintings in the series, are an extremely pessimistic portrayal of human relationships.